10699838

The People of the Great Circle

The People of the Great Circle

Prehistoric Mound-Builders in South Florida

Ted Ehmann

PINEAPPLE PRESS, INC.
Palm Beach, Florida

Pineapple Press
An imprint of The Rowman & Littlefield Publishing Group, Inc.
4501 Forbes Boulevard, Suite 200, Lanham, Maryland 20706
www.rowman.com

6 Tinworth Street, London SE11 5AL, United Kingdom

Distributed by NATIONAL BOOK NETWORK

British Library Cataloguing in Publication Information Available

Library of Congress Cataloging-in-Publication Data

978-1-68334-052-2 (cloth)
978-1-68334-053-9 (electronic)

∞™ The paper used in this publication meets the minimum requirements of American National Standard for Information Sciences—Permanence of Paper for Printed Library Materials, ANSI/NISO Z39.48-1992.

To Robin Fox, who first sparked my interest in anthropology and who later showed me the courage to communicate my views, no matter how unpopular.

Contents

Figures

Preface

Good work finds the way between pride and despair.
It graces with health. It heals with Grace.
It preserves the given so that it remains a gift.
By it, we lose loneliness:
we clasp the hands of those who go before us, and the hands of those who come after us;
we enter the little circle of each other's arms,
and the larger circle of lovers whose hands are joined in a dance,
and the *larger circle of all creatures,* passing in and out of life,
who move also in a dance, to a music so subtle and vast that no ear hears except in fragments.

—Wendell Berry, *What Are People For?*

There are many accounts of the mound-builders of North America. For over 150 years, anthropologists and archaeologists have probed their ruins and theorized about their origins. Millions of tourists have visited the county, state, and national parks to view their constructions and artifacts firsthand. I remember my first visit to Serpent Mound in 1992. Besides being struck by the engineering feat, I was overwhelmed by the humanity evinced by what was a profound religious place. Researchers have located the epicenter of the mound-builders as Ohio. By exhausted carbon dating of the earliest of these "Hopewell" sites, there is agreement that it all started to happen there in 200 BC. Following the material record, archaeologists have documented the spread of the culture, north, west, and south. None have successfully determined the reason the Hopewell culture disappeared after only seven centuries, around 500 AD. Twenty-five years after walking the ruins of the Midwestern mound-builders, I retired to South Florida. While reaching the numerous mounds near my home and the people who built them, I discovered that eleven centuries before Hopewell, the early Floridians had built the first burial mound in North America. Six centuries before Hopewell, the Floridians were building immense circular ritual spaces four hundred feet in diameter wider than St. Peter's Square in Vatican City, and mound/pond mortuary complexes. So what happened and why in my journeys had I never heard of the ancient mound-builders of southern Florida?

The story of the ancient mound-building societies in North America, I would discover, began with the building of a monumental earthwork complex of mounds and circular ridges built by hunter-gatherers in Louisiana. A thousand miles southwest of Ohio and fourteen and a half centuries before the origins of the Hopewell people, prehistoric people began engineering a regional ritual center. Carbon dating now confirms that centuries before the site was abandoned, and before Ohio, hunter-gatherers at the southernmost tip of North America were likewise altering the landscape.

In 1990, I journeyed to Moscow. I was part of a small but diverse group of Americans who met with a larger group of the then Soviet Union for a week-long conference titled The Seventh Generation. The reference was to a long established Native American view that all decisions pertaining to the people and the natural environment should be made considering the next seven generations. The first day of the conference, I noticed the Native Americans in our group had met up with the indigenous people of the northern region of the Soviet Union. It was the first time any North American tribal people met with the nomadic tribesmen of Siberia in modern times. The Soviet native people had only recently been forced to assimilate, a process in which the Soviet State took the young men to be educated in St. Petersburg and Moscow, a policy used a century before in the United States and Canada. This forced system would lead to the disintegration and termination of coherent, vital, and persistent hunter-gathering societies that were over 150 centuries old. Also, in 1990, author/farmer Wendell Berry wrote two short essays titled "Damage" and "Healing." In "Healing," Berry speaks of the two circles, the larger circle being all beings and the natural world, the world where humans are beings, nothing more, nothing less. Then there is the smaller circle within the larger one that is the human circle and our human relationships. His words have guided my every action and every thought since.

The genesis of this book was in research I began on the Calusa Indians, after moving permanently to Port Charlotte in 2016. I was attracted to the Calusa because of their wood-carving tradition. Unlike the researchers I will discuss later, I had no preconceived ideas or beliefs about the Calusa. Only when I was finishing my work did I realize my findings, my models and theories, would depart and differ dramatically from the existing and dominant view of the entire prehistory of South Florida. I believe that many of my conclusions contribute to a greater understanding of the prehistory of South Florida between 800 BC and the sixteenth century.

My entire life has been focused on my love of the humanities and my passion for anthropology. The wooden artifacts that drew me to the Calusa were the finest examples I had ever seen, and they live on only in the exquisite and beautifully rendered watercolors and drawings of the first to discover them in 1896. I believe American and world anthropology owe a debt of gratitude to Frank Hamilton Cushing and his artist assistant, Wells Moses Sawyer, who recorded and saved for posterity a record of a unique and very distinctive culture and set of beliefs. Later and beginning with her research and subsequent publication, Marion Spjut Gilliland, a respected curator, in 1989 painstakingly accessed and documented all of Cushing's finds from Key Marco. I am equally indebted to two archaeologists whose research on hunter-gatherers in the southeastern regions of North America helped me relate the Calusa to the entire epoch. George R. Milner's research on violence and warfare became a trusted reference. Likewise, senior Poverty Point researcher Jon Gibson gave me a reliable and commonsense-driven context for the cultures and behaviors of the Calusa and their neighbors.

Cushing was unaware of another culture inland that coexisted with the Calusa in southern Florida. He knew nothing of a large, persistent hunter-gathering culture who together with the Calusa engineered large ceremonial mound complexes with great circular ditches. Likewise, I started my research not knowing the unique coming together in a single long epoch. Cushing wrote pages in his journals about the unique environment that was South Florida, including the interior. Perhaps if he had not died suddenly a year after leaving Key Marco, Cushing may have returned to make such discoveries. Cushing was one of the first to excavate Calusa sites, and as such Calusa and prehistoric South Florida were a tabula rasa, a blank slate with no differing or competing views. This would change dramatically decades later.

Victorian Age–anthropologists like Cushing were big-picture people. While digging and later cataloging each significant artifact, Cushing made comparisons with other known cultures in the Americas who existed at the same time. He practiced his science before the modern techniques of carbon dating and subject specialization that characterize the field of anthropology.

I am of a similar mindset as Cushing and have always researched cultures and epochs in history in global contexts. From this perspective, I have been able to view the Calusa and their neighbors in relationship to what else was occurring and made manifest with humans around the world during the same time period, as well as part of a long human cultural continuum. Very soon into my research, it was clear to me that the Calusa, along with and because of their relationship with the Mayaimi and others, formed an extraordinary, atypical, and highly original regional culture. They also left a wealth of clues from linguistics to nonceramic artifacts that once unearthed and viewed in the proper context tell an incredible story. What occurred later in my research was it became clear that, although being one of the last groups in a wave of immigrants to South Florida from northern Louisiana during the Late Archaic period, the Calusa shared the same region with other people with the same language and similar beliefs and subsistence strategies. In short, there was much each regional player could build upon to assure stability and growth going forward. This coming together by 500 AD in the southern portion of Florida resulted in the largest group of significant monumental earthworks, villages, and sacred ceremonial centers yet to be recognized in North America. The monumental ceremonial complexes in South Florida were not the first in North America. Around 1800 BC during the Late Archaic period, ancestors of the Calusa built the only other monumental complex built by hunter-gatherers. The dramatic mound complex at Poverty Point in northeastern Louisiana (figure P.2) found its complete expression 2,200 years later in South Florida. The ruins along with a large number of ceremonial tablets with the unifying symbols of those people have survived to tell others of their incredible story.

Much of their mutual success can be attributed to the climate and the abundance of natural resources. Environmental research that dominates anthropology today confirms this fact. What I intend to illustrate is the success then, as today, relied more on shared beliefs, a spiritual unity that reassured a strong, confident identity and social order. Trade can only take a culture so far. The archaeological record is full of pre-Columbian native trade centers that lasted a century or two. At the center literally and geographically, the South Florida region was a series of monumental ritual landscapes. These centers held the people together, for generations. Historically such a record is an exception and not the norm.

Referring to the puzzle that is the Calusa and what occurred in South Florida, there has never been an attempt to pull data together. Those conducting the research have been specialists who also display obvious philosophical bias. Never in my research have I encountered anyone who was comfortable relating their data to data outside of their view or specialty. An example is the work by George Luer and Marion Almy on the southern Gulf Coast referred to as the Perico Island culture area. Both Luer and Almy live and work in Sarasota. They determined that despite the previous eighty years of archaeological data that showed a predominance of Glade ceramic types and shell tools identical to the Calusa, that there was a separate culture they cleverly called "Manasota," a combination of Manatee and Sarasota counties. Typical of the breed of Florida archaeologists post–John Goggin and William Sears, their attempts to establish a hitherto unrecognized culture went without sufficient peer review. A decade later, Jerald Milanich would accomplish the same feat when he brought into existence the "Belle Glade" culture in the Mayaimi culture area.

Seeing relationships, essentially a right-brain function, would help advance South Florida research. Without the process of connecting dots, and there are many, new research just adds to a pile of disconnected data and opinions. In South Florida, for two generations, the natural history wing of archaeology continues to control research and the narrative of prehistoric culture. Signaling a transition in 2011, Victor Thompson and Thomas Pluckhahn have established more accurate carbon dates for Fort Center, one of the region's major ceremonial centers. This was a major move in the right direction. Once a concerted effort is made to excavate Big Mound City and Big Circle Mound, we will all have a truer understanding of the region, its size, its people, and its legacy. The models recently put forth by A. Martin Byers claiming that the Hopewell and Mississippi mound-builders' cultures were built on preexisting stable social networks involving autonomous long-distant noncommunity groups are helping to paint the bigger picture of unique prehistoric cultures in North America. For reasons I will discuss in chapter 2, Thompson and Pluckhahn avoid naming the culture or people who engineered the monumental ceremonial earthworks at Fort Center and other places. Rather than being an oversight, a true understanding of the scale and scope of a Glades epoch in South Florida will require much more research. Also promising is the work of University of Florida graduate student Nathan Lawres, who focuses on the beliefs and spiritual practices of the people who built the monumental ceremonial and ritual complexes. The linguistics research by Julian Granberry in 2011 has supplied the missing piece to the puzzle and allows all who will follow to view South Florida as a single cultural region. Common to all these anthropologists leading the transition is their criticism of the abundance of specialty-driven research, a literature comprised of works by quite isolated and disconnected disciplines—archaeology, ethnography/ethnology, and physical anthropology. To this list I would add zooarchaeology and environmental anthropology. Granberry goes further, stating that such specialty intensification results in a general lack of training and adequate fieldwork experience. One thing I know from my research is that universities have not adequately taught their graduates to be self-policing of discernable bias and predisposition.

Ultimately, I have come to view this entire cultural epoch from 800 BC to 1700 AD in South Florida as one that was only possible by the coming together of distinct but related peoples. Using examples found elsewhere at the same time but in different regions of the world, namely the tribal areas in what would become "Europe" at the time of the early Holy Roman Empire and Christianity, I reworked my thesis to include the Mayaimi and Tequesta people working cooperatively with the newly arrived Calusa and achieving what few others had achieved in world history without internal warfare and continued strife.

The theoretical model, namely world history, established, I used the clues left behind by the Calusa and Lake People to prove and support the new model. I also used the archaeological reports and summaries that unwittingly prove my points when their intentions were clearly to prove the opposite. Archaeologists after 1949 gave the credit to the "Glades" people and other tribes they identified by pottery styles (figure P.1), and who anthropologist William Sears insisted did large-scale agriculture. Today, even though enough researchers disagree with Sears on the cultivation of maize and population centers based on agriculture, they share a less favorable view of the Calusa than the nineteenth-century anthropologists. The Calusa being fishing-hunter-gatherers and wood carvers, these modern anthropologists believed they could not have engineered the monumental works at Fort Center and elsewhere in the interior, despite evidence to the contrary. That conclusion can be disproven and overhauled by research on the Poverty Point, Louisiana, site.

Today, Poverty Point is not only a national monument, it also qualified as a UNESCO World Heritage Site. By comparison, the many monumental ceremonial sites of the Mayaimi and the Calusa in the Lake Okeechobee Basin, Florida, have had little to no protection or recognition. Protection and preservation of these and future sites is the bare minimum responsibility of the present generation of anthropologists, archaeologists, and the state. Once the sites are protected, then a plan to begin intensive archaeology by the right agencies and social scientists should commence. The only dual-

Figure P.1. Typical Glades Plain ceramic bowl. Photograph from the Peach State Archaeological Society of Georgia.

recognized UNESCO site, both cultural and natural heritage landmarks in North America adjoin the Okeechobee cultural and natural area that is the focus of this book. Ironically, it is also the only UNESCO site in North America on the "In Danger" List. Such world historical inclusions will transform these important sites into accessible centers for viewing and learning by generations of world inhabitants into the future. For now, the excavation of the other sites is critical to understanding what happened in pre-Columbian South Florida.

This book is a set of new eyes on the previous research and data and within an ever-changing global historical context. This book is essentially a history of a prehistoric subject. It follows a style of work I began as an undergraduate. I would select a subject and then create a symposium in writing on the subject. Each paper would have a variety of selected contributors to share ideas. The results were interdisciplinary responses from psychology, science, art, and religion to a particular historic subject. Therefore, this book is intended for the lay reader.

In the process of researching the Calusa, it became clear that Fort Center was a dedicated ceremonial complex that was constructed next to a sacred place. While terms like *ritual landscape* have been used by anthropologists and archaeologist since around 1980, the terms *sacred place* and *sacred space* are almost never found. The first use I have found in twenty-five years was in a paper by John E. Clark, "Surrounding the Sacred" (2004), that appears in a collection of papers addressing the issue of social complexity in early mound-builder societies in North America. Clark remarked:

> The decision to build Poverty Point in the place chosen probably had much to do with the earlier mounds making this a sacred place.

He later states regarding Poverty Point:

> An especially created space with ample room for public theater, laid out with cosmic numbers and perhaps celestial benchmarks, should be seen as a sacred place.

Clark clearly understands how early societies created sacred spaces, but he has not embraced the concept of a sacred place, which is why the people before Poverty Point built the early mounds at that river location (figure P.2). I am comfortable using the terms because people today still make pilgrimages to sacred places. It is what humans have been doing going back to the Paleolithic. A significant reason for me writing this book is to call attention to sacred places on the earth, their importance, and the need to protect them. Most of the sacred places in the Old World have been preserved and protected. All have

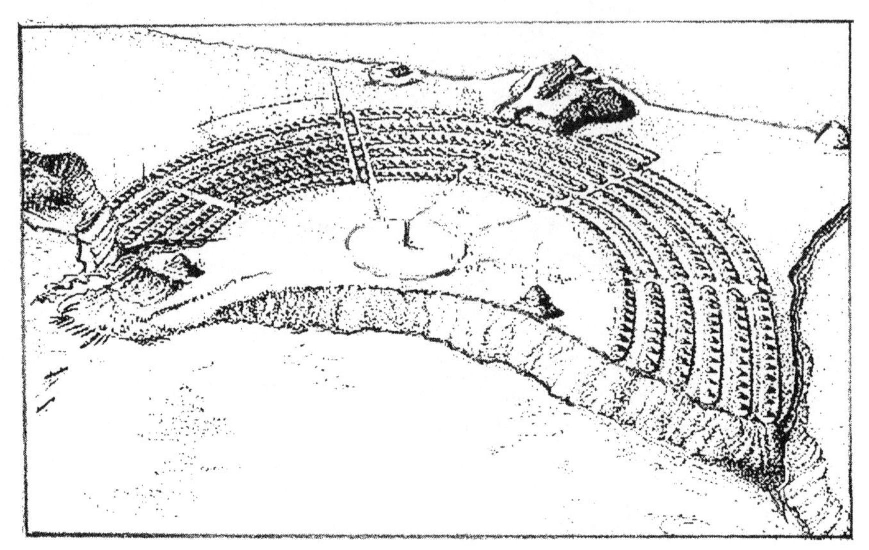

Figure P.2. Archaeological reconstruction of the Poverty Point archaeological site. From Jon L. Gibson, *The Ancient Mounds of Poverty Point* (2001). With permission from The University Press of Florida.

adjoining sacred places that have been recognized as World Heritage Sites by UNESCO. In the New World only one, Poverty Point in northeast Louisiana, has been so designated. The first known sacred place, Casma/Sechin Valley, Peru, has the Chankillo Observatory site pending, and the Great Serpent Mound in Ohio is also pending. Fort Center, near Lake Okeechobee, Florida, does not even have the designation of a National Historic Site.

Another important reason for this book, the subject of sustainable societies, makes the behaviors and social processes of the Calusa and Mayaimi people surprisingly relevant. They experienced population explosions, global warming, rising sea levels, and deadly hurricanes and still lasted collectively for twenty-five centuries. Many scientists have remarked on the interdependence of people with their environment. The holistic view was lived and passed on to each generation of Calusa and Mayaimi people. To quote Nathan Lawres, their world was a world of relatedness. I believe that Martin Byers's explanations of Hopewell social stability apply also to South Florida and were critical for the longevity of the Calusa and Mayaimi people. Could these prehistoric people provide answers to our most pressing global problems of climate change, scarcity of the essential resources for life, as well as minimizing social strife?

The Calusa and the Mayaimi have disappeared. They did, however, leave behind many clues as to their rich prehistory in South Florida. Separate and collectively, they reshaped the landscape, building phenomenal ritual spaces. These physical records are likewise disappearing at an alarming rate. What once was a densely populated region living off the abundant resources for thousands of years has but only a few surviving monuments to those achievements. Those few now suffer from neglect and apathy. If my research has taught me anything, it is the necessity of preserving and protecting the past for future generations. I was born in 1949. If I was raised in Florida, according to Gordon Willey's report of that year, the largest percentage of prehistoric sites had already vanished from the Florida landscape. By providing a historical narrative and drawing attention to the rampant destruction of archaeological sites, I hope to involve future generations to ponder the past and honor these prehistoric dwellers by preserving and sharing their history.

A word about my anthropological view. My passion for anthropology began in 1989. I purchased a used paperback copy of a book titled *Encounter in Anthropology* by Robin Fox. It was the best dollar I have ever spent; I was hooked. Subsequently, though an art and history major, I read every work by Fox. You will see me take on the majority of anthropologists in Florida in this book. We do not see the past in the same way. I believe, as Fox explains, that to know humans you should concentrate on the hundreds of thousands of years of human trial and error during the crucible known as the Paleolithic. I never did graduate work in anthropology. So, I have not been brainwashed by the progressives. Those who follow the German Romantics and their sociology-driven view focused on complex societies. The mound-builders in South Florida were hunter-gatherers long after their contemporaries moved in the opposite direction. It has been a joy discovering and sharing with other generations of humans who were the embodiment of our truest form and nature.

• 1 •

Florida's Best-Kept Secrets

At the middle of the twentieth century a great part, I should say well over half, of the archaeological sites of all types on the Gulf Coast of Florida have been seriously damaged or completely destroyed.

—Gordon R. Willey, *Archaeology of the Florida Gulf Coast*

The cultural tradition of the Calusa and their neighbors were deeply rooted in the Glades Tradition. Relying on aquatic resources, the Calusa developed a powerful tributary chiefdom prior to the arrival of the Spanish.

—Ryan J. Wheeler, *Treasure of the Calusa*

When Gordon Willey, on behalf of his study prepared for the Smithsonian in 1949, stated "the tragic destruction and loss of prehistoric sites," his study went no further than Charlotte Harbor. South Florida was still undiscovered and not researched. My research shows that South Florida's sites did not fare any better than those in the north. Likewise, when Luer and Almy wrote about the serious destruction of sites in my area in 1987, there has been only silence for thirty years.

When I moved to Charlotte County in 2016, there were no ancient mounds or villages that I could visit. Upon reading Willey's report, in 1949 there were an uncharacteristic five known Calusa Indian sites in the entire county: Cayo Pelau, Whidden Creek, Aqui Esta, Gasparilla Sound, and Hickory Bluff. In 2018, I requested from the Department of Cultural Resources the present number of known archaeological sites in Charlotte County. The number is now 205. Not only are the residents of Charlotte County unaware of the many prehistoric sites just minutes from their homes, the county officials have been equally unaware for decades.

The State of Florida guards its ever-increasing master list of prehistoric sites. For the past seventy years, they have failed to understand that all such efforts were too late. Past laws make it a misdemeanor to recover artifacts on state lands. Anyone who works with archaeologists and the state agencies are literally sworn to secrecy. The selling of Indian artifacts was and remains big business in Florida. While the policy makes sense, the fact of the matter is that every one of the thousands of sites dating from 10,000 BC were found and reported by the public. So, it's insane to think that the discoveries by the public can be kept a secret.

The state can only try to protect archaeological finds on state property. With the exception of the state's purchase of the Fort Center site in 1999, a significant world prehistory site and a site discussed often in this book, most state lands were designated many years ago. This means, as in the case of my county, Charlotte County, the majority of the 205 prehistoric sites are on private property. This makes the state's cultural resources even more valuable. Looting of artifacts on public lands became such a problem that Governor Rick Scott passed a law in 2013 that allowed the arrest for a first-time offense, along with up to five years in jail and a $5,000 fine. A sign of how much money is in the sale of antiquities, artifact looters and dealers lobbied the Florida legislature in 2016 to allow the taking of artifacts after paying $100 for a permit. Bill #803 got every archaeologist screaming holy murder to the deaf ears of well-greased representatives. As I will discuss in chapter 13, archaeologists and academics in general have been their own worst enemy. Collectively since the middle of the twentieth century, their behavior has been equally as opportunistic. They have used the excavation of prehistoric sites for personal gain and simultaneously allowed those sites to stay unprotected and exploited by developers. Even before Congress passed the National Historic Preservation Act of 1966, the solution can be found in British "common law." Common law formed the basis for the Public Trust Doctrine adopted by many states where lands are held in trust for future generations. Therefore, in Florida, not only the beaches and parks but also any sites and artifacts should be held in trust. There is no way that sites and artifacts, art of the public trust, should be allowed to be taken by individuals from the public and used for individual gain.

Florida's population has increased at an amazing rate. In 1950, for instance, when Gordon Willey reported the loss of over one-half of the known prehistoric sites, there were three million residents. By 1990 that number increased fourfold to twelve million. By the end of 2018, the population is estimated at twenty-four million people. When Willey made his conclusions, he wrote optimistically that there still will be for future archaeology all those unknown sites in the interior of the state. My research shows that many of the most significant archaeological sites will be in the counties surrounding Lake Okeechobee in the interior southern portion of Florida. Glade County had three well-known excavated sites by 1949. The state now reports that there are 341 additional sites. That means, due to the absence of state land, every one of those important sites are on private property. Glades County has no planning policy recognizing and promoting the 341 sites. Neighboring Hendry County has a total of 224 unexcavated, unprotected sites on private property. North of the lake, Highlands County has a record 352 sites, most on private property.

The prehistoric cultures thrived on the two shores and in the interior regions. The abundant tropical climate supported large populations. That is why, no matter where you live, there will be a village site, a cemetery, or a burial mound close by, and sometimes on your own property, something the current president of the United States discovered after he purchased Mar-a-Lago in West Palm Beach in 1985. Like dozens of other wealthy property owners in Palm Beach, such as conservative talk show host Rush Limbaugh, prehistoric sites often are right under your feet. Because of my research, I know of several residential properties currently for sale that have significant Indian earthworks on their front lawns. Currently there is a building lot in a wealthy gated community at Key Marco, Collier County, where not only do you get a private boat slip but also the oldest burial mound in the New World. Everything in Florida is available for the right amount of money. An old miniature golf course located on the Charlotte Harbor just sold for a record $80. A square foot.

Adding insult to injury, the records of these amazing sites for future generations were never created (figures 1.1 and 1.2). If you search online, you will find no mention of them. Prehistoric sites that received designations as National Historic Landmarks in Lee County have no information. All data and locations are blocked from view. It has become the policy of the government and the archaeologists to take their secrets to the grave. So a person with half a brain and some Internet search skills can locate any one of those sites and then drive there and visit them. It is also a terrible insult added to injury that a policy that allows cultural resources to die in secrecy does not have the social conscience to record the sites, record for posterity, a site they would not have known about without the help of the public.

A perfect example is what may turn out to be one of the most important sites in "world prehistory"—the Great Circle at the Fort Center archaeological site in Glade County. If you were to search for it online, you won't find it. A ritual circular ditch measuring 1,173 feet in diameter used to unify a lost civilization in South Florida has disappeared from science and from history.

Figure 1.1. Photograph of Mound Park, St. Petersburg, Florida, 1910. Materials used for road building. State Archives of Florida, Florida Memory.

Figure 1.2. 1909 postcard of Indian Shell Mound, Fort Myers, Florida. Materials used for road building. State Archives of Florida, Florida Memory.

Toward the completion of my research, I found a dissertation by a graduate student in anthropology from the University of Florida (1989), Jeffrey McClain Mitchem. His paper listed all the site information for many counties, including my own. I literally read in detail what had been hidden from the public for over a hundred years. The pages read like an obituary since all but a very few had survived repeated destruction and looting. Considering that they were kept top secret and still so, there must be a better way. What makes me angry is that the artifacts and details about the site went somewhere, but not anywhere that the people for whom the sites are in trust discover. Further, there is good reason to question this student's conclusions based on the exclusive information he was allowed to view. The student's view of what the archaeological data indicates was uncannily that of Dr. Jerald Milanich, a view that is quite different from what I believe the data supports.

As I will relate in detail in chapter 3, with all the so-called scientific research into the prehistory of South Florida and the region's various classifications and cultural chronologies based on ceramics, not one of them bothered to research the geology of the region. Had they done so, they would have discovered, as I did in 2018, that there are no clay deposits for the types of clays required for ceramics in all of the region. It turns out that South Florida is unique in another way in that it is only one of a very few clayless regions in the southeastern United States.

As you will discover from my historical accounts of South Florida archaeology, there is an increasing trend toward nonagreement. Since 1980, cultures, dates, and conclusions change dramatically. This shifting sand has been the result of the attitudes and philosophies of certain researchers. There are no final words, and thereby, many of the older sites, or at least their data, will need to be researched all over again. In the following chapters, I will show the differences in approach and conclusions between the independent and then government-initiated excavations in South Florida and the later ones by academics driven by personal agendas. There are differences of opinion—that is quite natural—but differences of motive are troublesome.

There has remained one dedicated and steadfast Calusa researcher, William H. Marquardt. He arrived in South Florida archaeology during the 1980s, and as such he is heir to those researchers at the University of Florida before him. To his credit, he collects data, a great deal of it. As a result, his theories and views have changed, as they should over time. He clearly is a present-day defender of Calusa "exceptionalism," and he more than all the other researchers combined has the data to prove it. While I am sure he will not agree with many of my theories and conclusions, I am confident that he approves of my effort to relate to the general reader what happened in South Florida before the arrival of the Spaniards.

I have brought to the attention of the reader some of the unintended consequences of keeping the prehistory of South Florida a secret. There is one more I feel needs to be addressed; namely, the sense of place and the source of community pride. A truly American voice, who more than most understands people and the land, Wendell Berry, once wrote that a healthy community had "memory." How a community, a place, embraces or does not embrace its past has been a leading indicator of that community's shared values. Today you see those values in the community's planning documents. Making room for the preservation of the past is an exercise in stating who we are today, and who we intend to be tomorrow. As I have traveled the world and visited both prehistoric and historic sites, I could not help but notice the less tangible, but significant, sense of place and sources of pride for those communities that had preserved their past. South Florida has more newcomers than it has residents with long histories. That has not, however, resulted in communities who have no interest in the past. Quite the contrary. I have found that often it is the newcomers who most desire the history and are open to the possibilities that are their new place. In chapter 12, I will discuss heritage tourism. Heritage tourists actively seek out places rich in history. Often, and this may be how it plays out in South Florida, it will be the outsiders who recognize the treasures buried in our backyards in Florida. I can only hope.

• 2 •

Bias and Predisposition in the Archaeology

Two hypotheses have been advanced for the function of these circles. They could have been ceremonial, as set forth by John Goggin and William Sturtevant (1964). This use is highly improbable, particularly the notion of any Calusa input for the ditches.

—William Sears, *Fort Center: An Archaeological Site in the Lake Okeechobee Basin*

However, Sears' total rejection of any ceremonialism associated with the Fort Center circle is premature, particularly when you consider the mound and pond feature of the Caloosahatchee circle.

—Robert Carr, "Prehistoric Circular Earthworks in South Florida"

South Florida has remained a very distinct environment since prehistory. When you consider the region's long, continued history of human habitation back to the Archaic period, it is reasonable to assume that a single dominant culture established itself there. Add to this view that because of the region being relatively remote to other nonpeninsula cultures during these periods, it is curious why anthropologists would later see smaller enclaves of culture dividing up the region. So, what happened? The subject never changed, only the researcher's viewpoint. According to the leading and most prominent anthropologists who have studied the prehistoric people of South Florida, there has been agreement for the past 120 years that these groups settled and occupied the southernmost region of Florida for the better part of seventy continuous centuries. They only disappeared in the seventeenth century when they succumbed to the diseases and other disruptive factors accompanying the arrival of the Europeans. Carbon dating of the relatively few excavated settlements out of many listed shows the Lake People arrived by 1000 BC, grew in numbers, and lived primarily in the savannahs, swamps, and forest near and around Lake Okeechobee in the interior. There is no agreement but plenty of facts that the Tequesta had settled on the nearby Atlantic coast and the Everglades. There is also agreement that the Calusa migrated to the southwest coast of Florida no later than 100 BC. Based on recent carbon dating at the Fort Center site, it is believed work began on the regional monumental ceremonial earthworks before 800 BC. This is just what agreement exists in the 120 years of study by those trained in such research. That and they made very plain ceramics.

For the past 120 years, anthropologists have recognized the Calusa and a Lake Area culture. Later they also recognized the Tequesta in the very southeast, and their northern neighbors, the Ais. Except for the Lake People, these groups did not have ceramic traditions. For this book, I will refer to the Lake People not as Belle Glades or Glades but by their more probable true name, the Mayaimi. In chapter 2, I will cover some of what I discovered about what can only be regarded as the invention out of whole cloth of a group of Indians living in the interior north in the Kissimmee River Valley, Lower Tampa Bay, and extending to the Florida Keys, now commonly known as the Glades after 1949. Prior, due to the work of John Goggin and Gordon Willey, the plain pottery made throughout South Florida was termed *Glade*, and had been associated with Belle Glades since the 1930s.

The Calusa first came to notoriety at the end of the nineteenth century by a renown British anthropologist who displayed their artifacts found in 1895, and later by the thousands of artifacts unearthed, recorded, and displayed also in Philadelphia the following year at the University of Pennsylvania Museum. One could say that the Calusa archaeological finds helped put the Smithsonian and University of Pennsylvania Museum on the map as world-class institutions. Florida anthropology and archaeology were suddenly important and significant. All things Calusa came to represent the best, most distinctive Native American archaeology in Florida. John Goggin and William Sturtevant stated as a result of their 1960s research that the Calusa had built such monumental earthworks as the ones at Fort Center. This is perhaps the last time the Calusa were credited with such substantial achievements until 2011. John Goggin concluded also that during that period, there was a single Glades culture region as well. After intensive archaeology in the 1930s, summaries of all excavations and resulting culture areas were published by Gordon Willey, and another by Goggin in 1949. This view of South Florida as a single Glades culture region for twenty-five centuries would later be fractured in the

1980s into many pieces. During the same time period, excavations decreased rather than increased. Today, we are living with the reworded pieces of a once logical and explainable view of pre-Columbian culture after 800 BC. Unlike the first archaeologists in Florida, site data is less likely to be correlated with previous or similar finds. Northern sites get preference over southern sites. Starting in the 1980s, the record reveals a discernable trend to lessen the importance of the Calusa in the pre-Columbian epoch, with one exception: Calusa specialist William Marquardt.

In 1994, Jerald T. Milanich published a comprehensive overview of Florida pre-Columbian archaeology. One can easily use his book as a history of the people and theories that have shaped the status quo and accepted views and theories. On page 277 he reveals one of the faulty assumptions held by academics pertaining to the prehistoric people in South Florida. He wrote:

> Indeed, the lifeways of the pre-Columbian native American Indians who lived in these southern regions after 500 BC were probably not too different from those practiced by many northern Florida societies.

A theory built on convenience but negated by archaeology in the south from 1896 to 1949 continues to make the South Florida epoch commonplace by interpretation.

William Sears's (1920–1996) research and 1982 publication of *Fort Center: An Archaeological Site in the Lake Okeechobee Basin*, marked the beginning by anthropologists to lessen interest in the Calusa while creating new culture regions and timelines. Since then, most new research in Florida has concentrated on the north and central sites, especially those in the Weeden Island and St. Johns River areas. Both Cushing and Sears viewed ceramics as the primary benchmarks for establishing prehistoric cultures after 500 BC. Ceramics appear on the first page of Sears's book, and thus it indicates his preoccupation. Ceramics have proven successful for establishing culture regions, fairly exacting dates for chronologies, as well as increases or decreases in trading. Early in my research, however, I soon realized that ceramics were very poor benchmarks for the Calusa and their neighbors.

I wish to state early on that I do not wish to speak ill of Sears. My critiques will be viewed as harsh. I do recognize that Sears's methods were in keeping with archaeology during that time. In order to advance a substantially different interpretation, each of his theories and conclusions must be addressed critically—something that the academics have been unwilling to do.

William Sears is the perfect person to begin the topic of bias and predisposition in the archaeological research in South Florida. He wrote in 1982:

> The Fort Center site seemed to be a good choice for the study of human cultural adaptation to a wet savannah environment. It was hypothesized, based on the presence of the linear earthworks at the site that the adaptation included a productive agricultural system to supplement or replace the food resources available through hunting gathering, and foraging (which I call "extraction"). For some time, I have been interested in the change from extraction to production.

It is clear that even before the work started, Sears chose Fort Center not to discover what happened there or to unravel its mysteries, but rather to make the subject fit his area of interest and support an already formed viewpoint about prehistoric cultures who engineered large, linear earthworks; that being that such cultures were incapable of such without changing over to productive systems (agriculture). It should be no surprise that Sears proved his theory, at least he thought he did. Sears on page 6 hypothesized that the most dominant earthwork at Fort Center was a "drainage ditch" (figure 2.1). Ironically, it was his student Robert Carr who later investigated another eight large, circular earthworks dispersed over the entire South Florida region. Several included known ceremonial elements. Despite Sears's subsequent work where he discovered only one to two families living at the site and his statements concluding that all individuals living there were dedicated to the construction of ceremonial earthworks, he still insisted that Fort Center was an agricultural village site, a view that is very seldom contested.

When Sears started his research on Fort Center in the 1960s, the concept of a Glade Lake-area culture was only twenty years old. There were only three sites and two teams of researchers. Sears took advantage of this and used the Fort Center research to establish its existence and develop a timeline of Glade periods using their simple utilitarian ceramics. He also used his conclusions to advance his career in academics and anthropology. These periods are still used today. He had to address the subject of the Calusa not only because they were known in the region as the engineers of great earthworks, but also because of their notoriety. In a classic display of bias, Sears again on page 5 wrote:

> Though there has been little study and certainly little published information, there has been tendency to assign these earthworks to the Calusa (Goggin and Sturtevant 1964), this implying a late date and to class them as "ceremonial." Even in advance of our fieldwork, neither of these ideas seemed acceptable.

Even when Sears discovered the inclusion of conch shells, an important Calusa symbol, he did not let any unintended facts sway him from his preconceptions of just what he would find there. This upfront and declared bias,

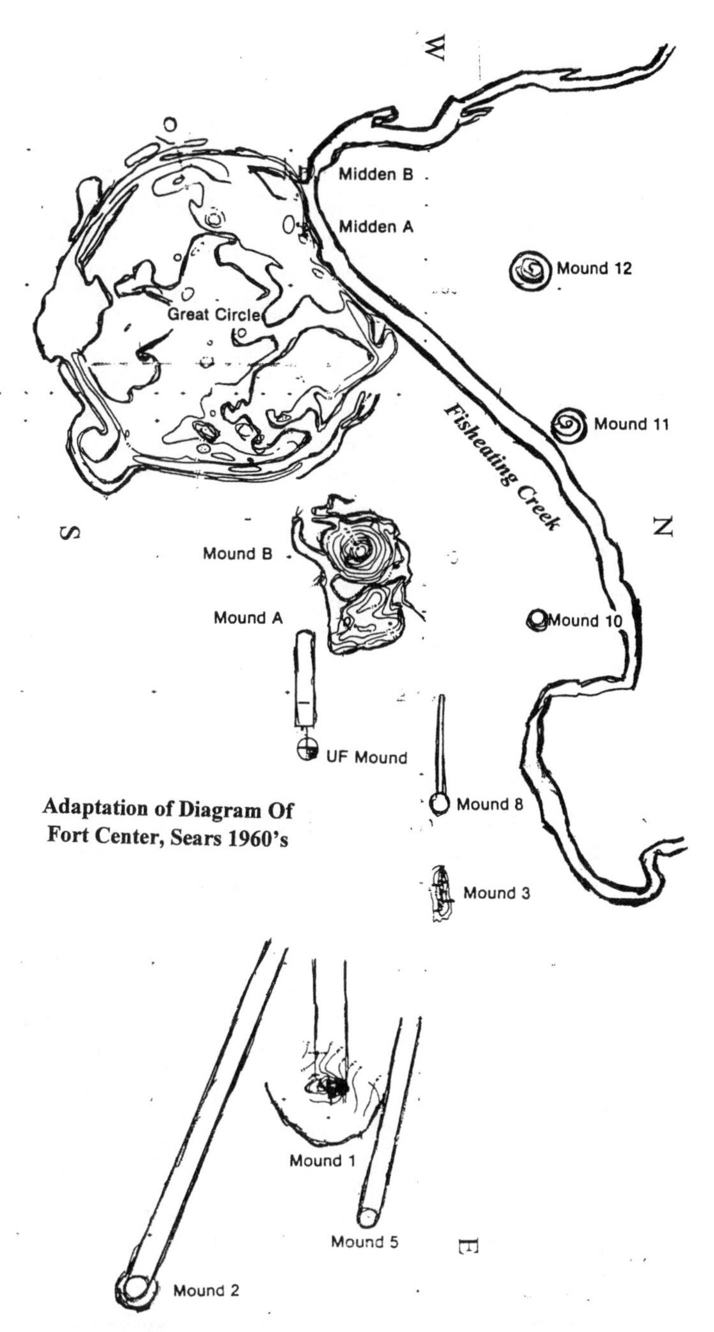

Figure 2.1. Diagram of the Fort Center archaeological site based on a map by John Furey of mound and features from Sear's excavation in the 1960s. State of Florida Board of Governors.

this arrogant foreclosure to all possible realities prior to research, is enough not only to disqualify his research but also disqualify him as a scientist.

Sears in his book contradicts his very own theory when he determined in the chronology that for almost twenty-five centuries only a few families lived at the site. He further characterized during his Glade II period (200 AD–900 AD) that "all of the people were involved with the operation of a ceremonial center." Even before his excavation and conclusions about Fort Center, anthropologists documented a long, persistent tradition of nonagricultural ceramic-producing cultures in the southeastern United States going back to 3500 BC. Therefore, Sears's emphasis was way off from what actually occurred. What was significant was first the construction of a large, circular ditch for rituals and a large mortuary complex with its pantheon of carved and painted animal and bird effigies unlike any the world had seen (figures 2.2, 2.3). Sears in his conclusion to the preponderance of wooden effigies displayed another faulty assumption about a relationship between his finds to Key Marco Calusa carvings. Sears wrote:

> I do not see in carving style or function, any real resemblance of relationship to the wooden objects from Key Marco, but I think that the choice of creatures represented and their apparent use do have similarities to another prehistoric North American Indian art. We can compare style and motifs with others that existed at the same time.

Had Sears followed through on this assumption, he would have discovered that no such wood-carving traditions except for the northwest coastal tribes ever existed. He would, after comparison with those groups, discover no similarities in either style or motifs. Sears, who argued often in his book about the insignificance of the unearthed pantheon of carved beasts and birds found at the Fort Center site, ironically agreed to a photo of one for the front cover of his book. Considering the bias displayed, one is led to believe that even the refusal to grant authorship of the Fort Center carved wooden effigies to the Calusa was a deliberate move to distance the site from the Calusa so that he could own outright and be known as the preeminent Glade archaeologist. Not to mention all the Calusa were known not to employ agriculture.

When Sears conducted his research of the Fort Center site in the 1960s, there was already a body of work from excavations of Glade and Gladelike sites from 1895 to 1945. Besides Cushing, Clarence B. Moore (1908) and the teams of federally funded excavations in the 1920s and 1930s had established cultural types and chronologies associated with a widespread South Florida culture. While Sears listed these works in his references, he never cited them in his research. This was extremely unprofessional. There has always been the requirement in archaeological research to relate new findings to the existing

Figure 2.2. Carved wooden figures excavated by Sears at the Fort Center mortuary/pond site with artist's rendering of original figures. State of Florida Board of Governors.

Figure 2.3. Carved wooden figures excavated by Sears at the Fort Center mortuary mound/pond site with artist's rendering of original figure. State of Florida Board of Governors.

research. This cavalier behavior on the part of Sears has resulted in a body of research that was and remains out of context. This problem I hope to correct in my work. As I will discuss in detail in chapter 3, when Sears moved to Florida, the state finally had, after one hundred years of archaeology, a working group of cultures and their sequence of dates (taxonomy and chronology). While still preliminary and subject to revisions based on new finds, using forced data from a single site out of hundreds, Sears and later Jerald Milanich would use this work to radically alter the existing cultures and sequences. The hijacking by these two major academics has so fractured a perfectly viable view that ever since it has become increasingly more difficult to make heads or tails of the twenty-five-century epoch.

Sears repeatedly made many significant claims of fact that were unfounded, contradictory, and never proven. He created four periods—Glade I to Glade IV—with dates. Sears would have us believe, for instance, that the Calusa, whose capitol was only fifty miles west of Fort Center, had little to no significant contact or involvement with Fort Center or the Mayaimi people from 100 BC to 1400 AD, a total of fifteen centuries. When he made this claim, all archaeologists knew of the Ortona mound complex just north of Fort Center and that it was where the Calusa built canals to connect the region to the headwaters of the Caloosahatchee River for the one-hundred-mile journey to the Southwest coast. Sears stated this knowing that the archaeology showed the Calusa were very active at neighboring Ortona during the dates corresponding to his Glade III and IV periods. Sears could find no cultural changes for the Glade III period, but he kept the period as "a necessary evil." Until now, I can only find a few established and respected archaeologists who will publicly disagree with his conclusions. Perhaps there has been little perceived benefit. The references cited in the back of his report were by anthropologists who researched the Hopewell prehistoric culture from 200 AD to 600 AD. If you were to do a survey in 1980 or even today, most researchers would generalize such earthworks as Hopewell in origin.

A year after Sears's book was published, Alabama anthropologist William McGoun wrote a book, *Prehistoric Peoples of South Florida*, in 1993, with the expressed intention of telling the story to the lay reader. Prior, all of McGoun's research was on the later mound-builders, the Hopewell culture that started in Ohio. Similar to Sears, he brought all of his preconceived ideas to the table. In chapter 4 of his book, titled "Earthworks and Effigies: Hopewellian-Related Societies around the Big Lake," McGoun, like Sears, also assumed with no other supporting evidence that Fort Center had to be the southernmost cousin of the Hopewell people. Amazingly, anthropologists had known for decades that the Calusa and Mayaimi lacked all the exotic mineral resources, raw or in artifacts associated with Hopewell villages. The earliest earthwork at Fort Center was the Great Circle, when new archaeologists redated the complex beginning in 2011. That construction was dated around 800 BC, one thousand years before the beginning of the Hopewell culture in the Ohio River Valley.

It remains difficult to understand the lack of challenges to Sears's village-with-agriculture hypothesis or McGoun's Hopewell-related theory. Sears had gone so far afield by basing his assumptions on William Denevan's archaeology at the time in the Amazon Basin, Colombia, that had people growing crops in geometrically shaped raised gardens, he totally ignored a more relevant site in a wet environment similar to Fort Center, Poverty Point, 1800 BC in Louisiana. Unlike Denevan's South American site, Poverty Point, first discovered in 1830, had been researched by several teams, and the findings were published by 1956. The answer seems clear. By comparing Fort Center with the best-known fifty-acre monumental earthwork center in North America built by fishing-hunter-gatherers, his hypothesis would be ill founded. In other words, not all large earthworks were the product of agricultural societies. McGoun's problem was another common trap. Not all mounds were built by the Hopewell or Mississippi societies. A similar trap has been assuming that mounds originated with the Mayans and Olmecs in Mesoamerica. Carbon dating shows that the mounds originated in North America, and I believe that both Sears and McGoun wanted to shift the limelight from the Calusa, who they anthropologically disregarded. If you want to divert attention, then create a new, shiny object somewhere else. The Belle Glade culture, unheard of prior, would do just fine for that purpose.

A decade after Sears stated he proved maize cultivation at Fort Center, anthropologist William Johnson published his findings on the soil at Fort Center. His papers in 1990 and 1991 proved definitively that the particular soil in the Fort Center area was ill suited to maize and any other crop cultivation. Professor Milanich, who had bit his tongue on the subject, finally admitted in his book in 1998 that the soil from Tampa Bay clear to the tip of Florida was not suitable for cultivating cultures. Ironically, he stated this to support a view of Tampa's Safety Harbor culture in another attempt to disenfranchise the Calusa from their northern regions.

Returning to Cushing and Sawyer, the first Calusa researchers, they too must have had the same faulty assumption pertaining to the carved and painted wood artifacts, but they never mentioned them in either of their detailed journals. I do not think that Sawyer could easily dismiss, like Cushing, these impressive wood carvings. This is evident in his painstaking watercolor renderings. The irony of all of this is that as far as the public goes, the most celebrated and most often viewed of Calusa artifacts are the wood carvings. The Key Marco cat, a carved, six-inch-tall statue that is part cat and human effigy, is one of the most popular displayed artifacts of North America in the

Smithsonian Institution. In 2008 to celebrate Twelve Decades of Archaeology, graduate students selected the Sawyer watercolors as the featured works at the University of Pennsylvania Museum anniversary exhibit.

Neither Cushing nor his predecessor, Lt. Col. C. D. Durnford, ventured any further than the islands, keys, and coastal areas of southwest Florida. That is, they never traveled inland. Cushing, however, in his journal accurately and beautifully describes the interior, but he never ventured there or talked to others about tribes and known archaeological sites. Even today, travel to those ruins is particularly difficult owing to the wilderness and wet terrain. I continue to wonder: What if Cushing had ventured there in 1896? Would he see what Sears and others saw, an entirely different culture, distinct from Calusa? Or, would he see what I see, the coming together of two cultures into an entirely new regional view and expression?

The late Archaic period in Florida, even for fishing-hunter-gatherers with no interest in large settlements based on agriculture, with the improved tropical climate and abundance of resources, witnessed an explosion in populations. Discoveries of important archaeological sites around the world, prior to, during, and after southern Florida's sites confirm this as a historic trend. Here again South Florida was unique, for it was home to a recognized and frequented sacred place dating back sixty centuries BP when smaller bands of Paleo-Indians called it home. In fact, I intend to argue, that the southern portion of Florida had such a wealth of natural and cultural resources, an abundance of such, that except for the northwest coastal region of the United States and Canada, and areas in the southern Pacific region, none could rival its abundance and its suitability for the role the culture region would play in the history of the Americas before Columbus. Maybe because the land was not suitable for growing crops it allowed the people to excel, formulating distinctive beliefs and ways, including ways of working and living together.

There is something unique to Florida anthropology that continues to influence research to the point where all that remains is a narrow, one-sided view of prehistoric people and events. Around the time of William Sears as curator at the Florida State Museum in Gainesville, state anthropology and archaeology moved into the Florida Museum of Natural History. What evolved was a shift from conventional cultural anthropology to historic ecology. More and more anthropologists availed themselves of the personnel, botanists, zoologists, and a new branch of archaeology headed by Elizabeth Wing, zooarchaeology. While Sears credits Dr. Wing for her help with faunal remains at Fort Center, a great opportunity was missed. Zooarchaeologists excavate and sample in order to provide all data on what the people at that site ate, a sort of "you are what you eat" scenario. Sears knew, or so he theorized, that the people ate corn. Had Sears utilized Dr. Wing to sample the large middens at Fort Center, we might have conclusive evidence that the Mayaimi people ate mostly fish.

The environmental wing of the Florida Museum of Natural History had such sway on the hypothesis going into fieldwork in South Florida that for two subsequent generations, archaeologists spent a disproportionate amount of money and time producing poor scholarship. One such example is the work of Randolph J. Widmer. In Widmer's book *The Evolution of Calusa: A Nonagricultural Chiefdom on the Southwest Florida Coast* (1988), Widmer stated that his work was to provide a synthesis of all Calusa research, since none existed. He also intended to use the Calusa to provide a theoretical model for a nonagricultural chiefdom. Widmer reveals his philosophical bias and predisposition in his preface on page xiv, as well as stating he will make "no apology," a point I will borrow for my work.

> In an ecological theoretical model as developed here, however, what appear to be incomplete archaeological data becomes very useful and "complete." Therefore, I make no apology for what may be regarded by many as pushing beyond the limits permitted by the data.

There was absolutely no reason for theorizing with limited data. As I stated earlier, Poverty Point, a famous nonagricultural chiefdom, had been thoroughly researched and published thirty-two years before Widmer's work. Even worse was Widmer concluded that because the Calusa society was dependent on fluctuating marine resources, they had no other option but to evolve into a strong, dominant, lineal-descent chiefdom. This view, painfully, is even believed by those few who have spent their careers specializing in Calusa archaeology. According to Widmer, because of the particular environment it will produce the needed political order. Again, Widmer never incorporated other fishing-hunting-gathering people around the world. Like Sears, if he had his intended conclusion, it would have fallen apart. For instance, if Widmer had read the anthropological research on the various tribes on the northwest coast of North America, he would have discovered a wide variation in political organization. Except for temperatures, the northwest coast archipelago is the most similar environment in North America to that of the Calusa. The societies were dependent also on fluctuating marine resources. The Nisqually people of Puget Sound had no inherited positions of power. A chief was chosen for his wisdom and knowledge. Their neighbors, the Tulalip, had a chiefdom identical to the Calusa power based on rank and status by heredity. The Quileute had no chief but chose to have house groups. The rank of house groups was based on their generous feasts. Inland tribes like the Nez Perce chose to have a chief for each band; in other words, many local chiefs all chosen from the elders in the group. Based on this one comparison marine environment, Widmer's assertions were absurd. True, the nonhuman components of a local ecology have encoded behaviors. The hallmark of anthropology, the study of the human component, is one of trial and error, winners and losers, the study of choices.

Anthropologist William Marquardt came to Florida and the University of Florida in the 1980s. He grew up in the environmentally influenced theories. Unlike any of his elders or contemporaries, Marquardt started digging and dating. Over decades, Marquardt is not only a believer in the uniqueness and exceptionalism of the Calusa, he has altered his views to accommodate what he has learned. First that the evidence shows "the possibility of significant migration from the Belle Glade area (near Lake Okeechobee) to the southwest Florida Coast" (2001). He also supports a very logical conclusion that the rigid hierarchical and complex social organization of the Calusa was a cultural response to the Spanish invasion of the sixteenth century. Prior it had many elements of egalitarian and less complex organization. Therefore, to settle the Widmer theory, it was not the environment or food shortages but invading Spaniards that caused them to be complex. Since the translation and publishing of Hernando de Escalante Fontaneda's diary, most researchers had a dislike for the Calusa as they believed them to be violent and fierce, when in reality they were forced into meanness, as it turned out. Marquardt appropriately states:

> Although the Calusa were far from isolated during the Woodland period, they expanded most visibly during the Early Mississippian (A.D. 1000–1200) increasing the size and height of their settlements, engineering, intrinsic and intensive waterworks of impressive proportions and trading in exotic materials with partners. Having partners in other regions would have had a distinct advantage.

Here, I have to bring in the recent theoretical models by Hopewell culture specialist Martin Byers. Closer to Florida than the northwest coast people, Byers believed that the Hopewell and later Mississippi people (who we know interacted with the Calusa) reestablished a long-standing and preexisting social organizational strategy. His theory of the Dual Complementary Heterarchical Community/Cult Sodality Heterarchy Model, when applied to South Florida, would indicate that the autonomous local community and chiefdom polity shared a social organizing system with an autonomous transient transregional polity. This complementary and dual-organizing strategy was far more complex than those theorized by Widmer. It was also far more stable.

Widmer has been but one of many brainwashed environmentalists playing at anthropology in South Florida. Florida anthropologists must learn that you are not taking chances when you use credible evidence of hunter-gatherer behaviors and choices elsewhere to theorize regarding the cultures in South Florida. Who knows, you just might get it right. Case in point, the Mayaimi or the Belle Glades or whatever name you want to give to the people around Lake Okeechobee. Not one of the anthropologists who has turned the spotlight on this extinct culture has ventured forward with any theory as to their social organization. Regarding the Calusa, they rely on sixteenth-century accounts. What if the Calusa were organized completely differently from, say, 500 BC to 1250 AD?

I cannot say enough about Cushing and Sawyer. Without their keen minds and talents, all would be lost regarding the Calusa. But even Cushing and Sawyer with all their excitement and enthusiasm missed what was right in front of them. By that I mean those possible aspects and achievements that distinguished the Calusa from the Mayaimi and hundreds of other ceramic or nonceramic-producing tribes in the Americas during this transitional period. Cushing's written accounts, maps, and drawings from the 1896 Pepper-Hearst expedition along with Sawyer's life-saving watercolors of the painted, carved, wooden artifacts got a great part of the story right for generations after, to read and understand. Ironically these two open-minded Victorian explorers missed the significance of two key aspects of the Calusa that made them unique and unlike their peers. Both great minds missed the two aspects that were literally right under their noses; namely, their engineering skills that included artificial ponds, lakes, and canal systems and their wood-carving achievements. What my research will show about the above-mentioned aspects of the Calusa material culture were highly distinctive. Most of the researchers who have followed in Cushing's footsteps such as Sears have repeated this same oversight and have done so contrary to the evidence that is clear and right under their nose. Sears and his contemporaries made the same mistakes regarding their engineering feats and wood carvings. Sometimes, when you research a people and a place, you find nothing that is good news. The fact that the Calusa had no ceramics and the Mayaimi people had common, utilitarian ceramics was good news. How you might ask? Well, it made them very unique. If they had such, they would be just one of many in Florida. The material record reveals that they deliberately, culturally chose not to be fancy ceramic producers. They chose it because their unique identities had different priorities. Hard to swallow when you're a real pottery hound.

Sears and those archaeologists who have followed insist that trade had to be the basis for the growth of the Fort Center site. Here again, Sears's own words contradict this entire scenario.

> All the non-ceramic artifacts recovered were manufactured from exotic materials. The Okeechobee Basin while rich in subsistence resources, is poorly equipped to supply raw materials to a sophisticated technological

> system. The Belle Glade people were forced to operate their adaptive systems as well as their elaborate ceremonialism with imported materials and finished goods.

There Sears stated that the Belle Glades had huge trade deficits lasting centuries. That could only be possible if they could offer their trading partners something better. Again, regarding the resource-poor Glade people, Sears and his contemporaries would have us believe that they would have little to no interactions with their resource-rich Calusa neighbors for twenty-five centuries.

Sears, Milanich, and so many other researchers should have their research questioned. In their haste to dramatically alter the established view of South Florida prehistory, there remain abundant data that could possibly fit, no matter how they try to skew or manipulate it. First and foremost, there are the canal systems found in every one of their new and separate culture regions. Everyone knows that they date to the Calusa, and the majority were in their "culture region." Their answer is just to ignore them. This really won't work since they are so much of the record now.

There is great promise to the academics and the lay people as well as in the information produced in this decade by newcomers to Mayaimi and Calusa research. First, anthropologists such as Thompson and Pluckhahn and Lawres and Colvin do include cross-cultural comparisons. When they theorize that South Florida is a distinct cultural area, they support that view by locating comparative cultural regions in world history. Second, they all have resisted the environmental bandwagon, which while it guarantees more funding and notoriety, it has produced some very awful scholarship in the area of cultural anthropology. There remains only one obstacle in the path going forward for these cited anthropologists. The intensive excavations of both Big Mound City and Big Circle Mound will be required to support any and all theories based on the Fort Center site. This missing information has kept Sears and other Glade archaeologists from having all the required supporting data for thirty-six years. As in the case of McGoun and the Hopewell influence on Fort Center, all you need is a few new and different dates and it's back to the drawing board for literally hundreds of previously reported "facts."

• 3 •

Decades of Disagreement and Disregard

> There is a third much more ancient Florida. This is a place that is often forgotten, downplayed or actively denied in recent grand narratives.
>
> —Neill J. Wallis and Asa R. Randall, *New Histories of Pre-Columbian Florida*

> It means that rather than it being consciously done as part of a collective, corporate activity in which it is seen as a small but necessary contributing part, it has to be exalted into an individual achievement to legitimize promotion and enhance status. The best way to do this is to specialize like crazy. The smaller the intellectual pond, the bigger appears the academic fish.
>
> —Robin Fox, *The Challenge of Anthropology*

My task has been to formulate some kind of narrative where the Calusa and the prehistoric people of South Florida, 120 years after Cushing left Florida, are viewed in a local and global context. This is what the earlier anthropologists were attempting to do. After all those years, due to the specialists, the accomplishments of these fishing-hunter-gatherers have gotten lost under piles of incidental research. Not only is their legacy being lost, but their humanity as well.

In researching for this book, I discovered that it was very difficult to find copies of twentieth-century South Florida archaeology books. I was fortunate to find a copy of Gordon Willey's eight-hundred-page *Archaeology of the Florida Gulf Coast* (1949). Thanks to his incredible work, I have a complete listing and description of all known sites as of 1949. Willey's complete catalog reveals all of the major archaeological sites that have totally disappeared in the last ninety years, but by accessing the master file in Tallahassee, you can see the incredible increase in known sites since 1949. It is important to note there were few interpretations back then, just data. I have done my best to reflect the style of research they conducted as well as the predominant philosophical viewpoints they employed. Milanich, in his comprehensive overview *Archaeology of Precolumbian Florida* (1994), begins with the pronouncement: "The growth of archaeological research since the 1960s has been phenomenal." The truth of the matter is, there was an intense competition that began in the late 1940s for status, fame, and notoriety—"big fish, small ponds." That new age in Florida archaeology began with the creation of the Department of Archaeology at Florida State University in 1948 and a separate Department of Anthropology at the University of Florida a year later. John M. Goggin was named chair of the University of Florida, Anthropology Department, and it was Goggin that defined all the cultural areas in the state and assigned the chronological stages for each of the cultures. Milanich recounts:

> Many of the regional cultures recognized today in Florida were Goggin's taxonomic constructs.

In the same chapter he states that Goggin had a "monopoly." When you consider that in 1948 there was very little literature on which to base the establishing of such a monumental task as well as very little scientifically conducted archaeology, how could one person within a two-year span accurately and reliably accomplish the region's chronology and taxonomy for the entire prehistory of the State of Florida? The answer is simple. No one could possibly do that task with any reliability. So, this new age can be characterized by men with incredible egos who could do and say anything because there was little previous scholarship to refute their findings.

Perhaps what will come to be considered one of the most faulty assumptions in American archaeology occurred in South Florida. In July 2018, I concluded my investigation into the existence of ceramic clays in the geology of South Florida. Referencing the entire literature and a 1949 Florida Geological Survey on Florida kaolins and clays, a 1980s US Geological Survey, and Florida county mining databases, I proved conclusively that there are no suitable clay deposits in the entire region. It turns out that the entirety of South Florida lies south and off the Gulf Coastal Plain. The Gulf Coastal Plain has rich, abundant, and very accessible deposits of fine, ceramic-type clays from Texas up to New Jersey. In defense of John Goggin, the father of South Florida ceramic types, these surveys were not available to him. Goggin, like Sears, Ripley Bullen, and Milanich, all did archaeology in the clay-abundant northern Florida regions. Goggin studied and worked in pueblo clay–rich New Mexico when he wrote the very first studies on South Florida pottery types. Eighty years later, however, there are no legitimate excuses for the archaeological brain trust at the University of Florida and the Florida Museum of Natural History to have missed such an important scientific fact. The implications are huge. My investigation proves that twenty-one separate and distinct types of classified ceramic types associated with South Florida were actually produced elsewhere and exported to the region. Because Central Florida likewise is affected, other ceramic types such as Pinellas, Pasco, and Safety Harbor equally come into question.

Also, around the same time, William Sears joined the faculty of the new archaeology department at Florida State University. Milanich states that by the mid-1950s, Bullen, Charles Fairbanks, Goggin, Griffin, Smith, and Sears were all doing archaeology in Florida. To assist their efforts, these archaeologists did a mad dash to find and list archaeological sites on the state's master file. With very little Florida-specific literature, except for Willey's work, to reference, all the mentioned archaeologists used the wealth of Hopewell data and literature (pre-Byers) to support their work and conclusions, interpretations not made by archaeologists prior to 1950. After all, they concluded, the mounds discovered all over Florida must have been related. This was a faulty assumption, which has, along with the redefined culture regions, chronology, and taxonomies, gone uncontested to this very day. Specifically, important to my research and this book is that Sears's references cited at the end of his 1982 Fort Center account of his 1960s archaeology has a total of eighty-two references, of which eleven are his own work. As I stated before, most of Sears's references had to do with Hopewell archaeology. All of the earlier archaeologists were also familiar with the Hopewell types, yet none determined that the mounds and types in South Florida were connected to the Hopewell culture.

Another drawback in researching the Calusa was that the Calusa artifacts have been literally scattered to the four directions. They are in collections not available to the public. Beginning with the first Calusa expedition by British archaeologist Lt. Col. C. D. Durnford in 1895, the artifacts unearthed, which included wood carvings, were whisked off to the British Museum in London after a brief stop in Philadelphia. The thousand-plus artifacts unearthed and cataloged by Cushing, hundreds of photographs, Cushing's journals, and Sawyer's watercolors of the celebrated carved and painted wood carvings were divided between the Smithsonian in Washington, DC, and the University of Pennsylvania Museum in Philadelphia. Later, some artifacts and Sawyer's notebooks ended up at the University of Florida Museum in Gainesville, and the majority of Cushing's drawings of hundreds of carved wood artifacts were donated to the Brooklyn Museum and others to the Haffenreffer Museum of Anthropology at Brown University. Except for but a few on display and a few others reproduced in books, these treasures remain buried now in storage. A twelve-foot-high carved wooden owl in the Calusa style unearthed in Hontoon Island far to the north now greets visitors at a center near Jacksonville, Florida. The owl was most probably a gift to a chief there, but an anthropologist has credited it to a much smaller tribe in the north with no wood-carving tradition.

Regarding the few published works on the Calusa, there are three written by Marion Spjut Gilliland, *Key Marco's Buried Treasure* (1989)—which beautifully illustrates the Calusa wood-carving tradition while the text concerns itself with the trials and achievements of Cushing's expedition; *The Material Culture of Key Marco*, Florida (1975); and *The Calusa Indians of Florida* (1996). Another work about the Calusa is by Ryan J. Wheeler, *Treasure of the Calusa*, self-published in 2000; Wheeler cataloged and revealed many unseen Calusa artifacts. It was an attempt to push a single Glade region for South Florida with the Calusa, a small subculture. He and I agree on a restoration of a single culture region but differ greatly in the how, what, and why. The most recent book, *The Calusa and Their Legacy: South Florida People and Their Environments* by Darcie A. MacMahon and William H. Marquardt (2004), while valuable for its reproductions of Calusa artifacts, adds nothing new regarding this unique culture. The author's texts are brief and cursory, lacking the curiosity and imagination of the Calusa's first researchers. It is essentially a textbook published to coincide with the new exhibit at the Florida Museum of Natural History featuring the Florida tribes with an emphasis on their environment. Finally, there are the works of Jerald T. Milanich, who has had the more difficult task of selling the public on a job well done while knowing that the archaeology of pre-Columbian Florida has favored the northern counties. In short, the story of Indians in Florida is literally top heavy.

Recently, there has been a great deal of interest, research, and theories regarding what is referred to as *transegalitarian* societies in the southeastern United States. The building of monumental ceremonial shell rings, some which existed in Florida during the Late Archaic period, has prompted questions as to the necessity or not for the society to have a complex political system. Considering that all settled fishing-hunter-gathering groups were believed to be egalitarian and without social ranking, those like the Calusa and Mayaimi in Florida do not conform to this model. Socioeconomic systems of early coastal subsistence cultures are heavily debated. Widmer's look at the Calusa was actually one of the earliest attempts to address the subject. As I have stated, statements like the following by Widmer can be totally disproven:

> The coastal adaptation as seen in southwest Florida is neither unique nor unusual, and in fact, corresponds precisely to sociopolitical expectations derived from studies of cultures utilizing other subsistence forms.

Expectations equaling predetermination amounted to poor science. Moving to the Mayaimi people, if you accept the commonly held post-Sears view that the (Glade) Mayaimi people, hunter-gatherers, with limited resources, built those persistent monumental earthworks around Lake Okeechobee, independent of the Calusa leadership, then how were Mayaimi organized politically? Here is a classic example of what I refer to as decades of disregard, one of the most important aspects of culture that has been mostly disregarded by Florida anthropologists and archaeologists. This is why I had to move outside of Florida for answers. It is likewise an example of bias as well as predisposition. What facets of a culture will be explored is decided by the interests and philosophy of the researcher, as I have shown with William Sears. In America, the early historical ecologists in anthropology insisted that neither culture nor the environment was the "sole determinant for change in human societies." However, as you can see in South Florida with Sears, the environment had come to be the sole determinant. So why research the subject of political authority and organization of the Mayaimi people? They built extensive monumental earthworks. They did extensive agriculture. They were essentially Hopewellian centers. They must have had a strong chiefdom, right? Not necessarily.

By the 1990s the view that humans were causing global warming prejudiced archaeological views totally to the environment. In Florida as elsewhere, climate change concerns and environmentalism were the new religion and dominant belief system. Calusa researcher William Marquardt is a classic example. He and his team revisited the Pineland Calusa complex to disprove the "cultural materialist" model set forth by Randolph Widmer, a model that argued that the social structure and symbolic ideational aspects acted as regulating mechanisms within the Calusa cultural system as a whole. Marquardt wanted to prove that the environment experienced changes such as rising and falling sea levels, which resulted in shortages and upheaval leading to a centralized political power—as I recounted earlier, a view not supported by other native cultures dependent on marine resources. Nor did Widmer have data from digs for support. At a time when the money and time would have made a difference in answering more significant and persistent questions, Marquardt produced a 935-page book that sea levels were not constant in southern Florida over a long period of time. This is all possible because the only grants and funding today is for research that focuses on politically charged "global warming" and "climate change." Another example is Dorothy Block, a Palm Beach Belle Glade culture specialist. Because of the Everglades environmental crisis and fears of rising seawaters threatening the expensive real estate on the Atlantic coast, interest and money for their archaeology has increased substantially. To these professionals, it really does not matter that no more is known of the Mayaimi people today than ninety years ago. They also benefit from a multiple culture versus single, regional culture view winning out in South Florida. If you do not think that there are politics between archaeological camps, think again. Some disagreements based on philosophical differences or just plain matters of interpretation are always present. Matters of turf and competition for funding are also a part of research today.

The Florida Public Archaeology Network, the largest educational outreach and site preservation organization, can testify to the benefits of stressing environmentalism over historic preservation and cultural anthropology. "The oceans are rising, the oceans are rising" brings in new volunteers and funds to a dying social science trying desperately to be relevant. Sociologists were never comfortable with the study of less complex hunter-gathering societies. Cultural relativism dominated a significant period in anthropological research, making the discipline irrelevant to the majority of thinking people. The pressing questions are still out there to be answered. While Florida archaeologists fight over their interpretations of the same data, no new discoveries are explored or reinterpretations attempted. The thousands of sites on the state master file have been ruined by years of development. Their demise is the byproduct of generations of archaeologists spending no time to argue for their protection. Rising sea levels centuries ago will never give us the answers to the big questions: Who were these people and how did they succeed in maintaining a continuous fishing-hunter-gathering culture in North America for twenty-five centuries? The answer was in the 1452 interior sites in South Florida that were squandered over the past seventy years.

As I stated earlier, the entire chapter in world history known as the Neolithic begins with the spiritual world, the beliefs, rites, and ritual landscapes of hunter-gatherers. The coming together of diverse bands to participate in community activities like worship, sacrifices, and burials had economic rewards not only for the religious sect, but as we discover early, also for the political elite. As Lionel Tiger and Robin Fox so beautifully illustrated in their research of basic human "bio-grammar," all modern-day forms of economic systems have their origins in the trial and errors of hunter-gatherer societies. Besides the foremost necessity of a culture to successfully adapt to the natural environment, the corresponding system of give and take, redistributing wealth, divisions of labor, and the forming of economic alliances was essential for the peaceful continuity and longevity of the culture/civilization. Systems of give and take have been treated by researchers in Florida in rather predictive, utilitarian, and simplistic ways. Sad state of affairs considering that economics along with sex are areas where humans excel and where human societies show incredible variation and creativity. Jon L. Gibson has highlighted a particular debt system that he believes was integral to the first mound-building societies, "the debt of gratitude." Totally applicable to the Calusa/Mayaimi monumental mound complexes, Gibson believes that supernatural gifts such as life's joy and spiritual protection were perceived/treated by the people in those early societies as powerful gifts given to them by the religious leaders. The corresponding debt of gratitude was more powerful and emotional than the commonplace exchange of gifts between two individuals. The repayment of the gift of gratitude was their dedication and labor required to build the large ceremonial mounds. Beliefs and symbols were as powerful then as today as organizing tools, the old "mind over matter." The Calusa and their neighbors experienced a very long existence, especially compared to civilizations like the Sumerians, Egyptians, the Olmecs, Mayans, and Aztecs. While historians focus on these early Neolithic experiments, they fail to credit the more successful societies in the New World, such as Casma Valley, Poverty Point, and the Calusa/Mayaimi cultures. While they argue that social complexity based on social inequality was the power behind the great mound projects, they have lost sight of the power of human beliefs.

Marion Spjut Gilliland, a contemporary of Sears, did not agree with him and supported a view of the Calusa as a major player in South Florida. Most have interpreted the socioeconomics at play in South Florida as a mirror image of feudalism in Europe during the Middle Ages. Like many anthropologists, Gilliland's views were based on European accounts, which described the paying of tribute by all tribes to the Calusa chief. Those same accounts do not describe the generosity of the Calusa leaders or the degree of gratitude by those paying tribute. I am convinced, however, that in order to be the hereditary leaders of fishing-hunting-gatherers for twenty-five centuries those under them must have had debts greater than the Calusa. As I illustrated earlier, feudal Europe had a very short life. Like their predecessors, the Roman Empire and the Roman Catholic Church, the economic system of Medieval Europe was more take than give. Recent research has found documents showing that the Church actually paid many of those who labored to build the great Gothic cathedrals. It has long been known that the clergy would sell indulgences to potential financial patrons for their help to build the cathedrals. This practice had a short life and was found by many to be a corrupt religious practice. After comparing the Calusa with other long-lived fishing-hunter-gatherer civilizations who occupied resource-abundant archipelagos—the Jomon in Japan, the South Pacific Islanders, and the tribes of the northwest coast of North America—they all prospered under a system of more give than take. The Calusa leadership became established, powerful, and influential because of their generosity.

The potlach, the occasional gift-giving feast employed by many indigenous people especially in the abundant archipelagos, must have played a major role early on in South Florida. Before the arrival of the Calusa, a previous culture that buried their dead in mounds and build large shell rings for ceremonies and feasts lived for thirty centuries on Horr's Island next to Key Marco. The Mayaimi people and their neighbors probably also built large, ceremonial works out of shells on their way to engineering the larger earthwork circles like the one at Fort Center for such feasts and festivities. The seasonal gift-giving feasts were also used for funerals and burials, weddings, adoptions, transferring title or land, and cementing alliances. No different from our modern-day societies where religious rites give room to social occasions. The Calusa recognized that in order to have power and influence they had to establish themselves physically and spiritually at Lake Okeechobee, and the ceremonial mound complexes were the way to achieve this. The ornate mortuary complex they created has no other like it in the world. Everyone has to die, and preparing the remains, performing the rights, and conducting the burials was big business. Families and the spouse needed the goods to afford the proper burial. The large, seasonal burials at Fort Center were labor intensive, expensive, and required the labor of many people. People had to be housed, including visiting dignitaries and elites. Feasts before and after had to be prepared and all accounts settled or credit established. While the models put forth by Martin Byers were not applied to Florida, it makes perfect sense that an autonomous, complementary religious cult had much to do with the building of and operation of the mortuary mound complex at Fort Center. Such an arrangement would have been an egalitarian carryover from the trial-and-error experiences of strictly hunter-gathering societies.

William Marquardt probably has written the most about the Calusa. If anyone has been responsible for the current historical narrative about the Calusa society, he is the one. The small amounts he has written regarding the Calusa chiefdom are totally derived from biased European firsthand accounts. You will not find him weighing such evidence against other chiefdoms at the time. His most troubling description of the Calusa chief beginning in 1513 AD was as follows:

> a powerful despot who was feared throughout Florida.

This value-laden term *despot* used exclusively to describe a tyrannical and oppressive leader in Europe lacks all objectivity. The Calusa leader and those that followed had never faced another race and a people who would not pay tribute. A family of leaders who had successfully led the people of a region for twenty-three consecutive centuries could never have historically been tyrannical in how they dealt with the people. I contend that viewing the Calusa leaders in the context of fishing-hunter-gatherer societies as well as the geographic size of their chiefdom, the Calusa leaders were just as fierce and violent as the situation called for. So far, there is no archaeological evidence of continued conflict to support the Marquardt description.

Again, I believe the work on the other Eastern Woodland moundbuilders and their complex social organization by Martin Byers need to be considered when investigating the Calusa. Those Europeans who wrote about the Calusa would not have been privy to or free to have recognized the complex strategy employed for social organization and social stability. I contend that Byers's model could apply to the Calusa. The Calusa were an Eastern Woodland people. The Calusa's dates correspond to the Hopewell's reemergence of the dual group strategy as well. Therefore, it was more than likely that at prearranged times and at cooperative and joint mortuary and burial mound sites, transient members from outside the region were present, and paid tribute in South Florida. Accordingly, those transient cult members within the Calusa polity journeyed to similar sites outside of South Florida, a complex system that Europeans would have no experience to be able to locate or study.

Much of the confusion surrounding the past 120 years of researching the Calusa and Mayaimi comes from insufficient models and incomplete research. When opportunities for detailed archaeology presented themselves, the wrong person for the job was entrusted with the task. Despite losing so much archaeological discovery to rapid development in the twentieth century, many important sites, especially in South Florida, were ripe for addressing major questions regarding who the people were and the details of their cultures, questions about their similarities or differences from other aboriginal cultures of that time. By employing narrowly focused, environmentally charged researchers, we have detailed analysis of some trees and no sense of the forest. Now a century later we have no idea who the "Glade" people were. When my research on clays in South Florida proved negative, I concluded the ceramics that once defined the people of South Florida were all imported. As Gordon Willey suggested in 1949, it would be wrong to believe that the "final word" so far in Florida archaeology is actually the final word. While the historic ecologists were analyzing every bone and pollen sample in the vast middens of the Mayaimi people, burial mounds, a critical source of locating the beliefs and corresponding social components, were ignored. The same goes for all Calusa sites. If it was not for Cushing's detailed excavation of the Key Marco site, our understanding of the people would be equally as sketchy, and few acknowledge his work.

Disregard for detailed archaeology of burial mounds and sites in Florida has been commonplace since 1949. Early archaeologists like Clarence B. Moore and Frank Hamilton Cushing made detailed notes for each burial mound. From those details, all researchers can see differences and similarities by which to establish precise taxonomies. From Moore's work, you can view each mound in a cultural and chronological context. Sears excavated a large burial mound at Fort Center. As I stated before, he found artifacts like pairs of conch shells and made no comment or analysis. Cushing excavated a large burial mound, the Safford Mound at Tarpon Springs in the Weeden Island culture area in 1896. Besides the largest cache of ceramic artifacts from one excavation, Cushing's data was rich for use as an ethnology revealing beliefs and social structure of the Weeden people. There have been no comparable data for post-1918 Glade and Calusa archaeology. Sears at the Fort Center burial mound found many turtle shells that had been altered. Again, no comment or analysis. At least they were significant clues to the Mayaimi people. More than likely, they were significant clues to hegemony with Calusa beliefs and practices. They were also clues to the size and duration of the South Florida culture. As Willey concluded, even in 1949, you cannot go back and revisit the sites. They are gone forever.

Wheeler agrees with my points on the importance of burial site data. In his 2000 book on the Calusa, he also expressed displeasure with the little amount of credible burial mound excavations. Working with such limited data, he made interesting comments on the few, but revealing, burials of women. His research shows that the Calusa and their neighbors held women in esteem. This is the proper use of burial data for the development of ethnographic understanding. True, there are ethical considerations when working with human remains. I do advocate for further research of skeletal data like the work done by George Milner.

I have only found one such Florida burial mound project in the archaeological research so far. A graduate student then at the University of Florida, Jeffrey McClain Mitchem, in his 1989 project for his dissertation detailing the findings at a later site of the Safety Harbor period, titled *Redefining Safety Harbor: Late Prehistoric/Protohistoric Archaeology in West Peninsular Florida*, provided a detailed and useable analysis of late period burials of the Tocobaga people of the Tampa Bay area. The distinct burial mounds at Big Mound City and Big Circle Mound, both critical for Sears's or my theories, have laid in wait now for sixty years. Burial mounds left behind by both groups in southern Florida could provide the much needed data and cultural timelines. Burials could have provided by now the much needed information on the transition from the earlier archaic inhabitants and the possible origins of all the groups that shared the region. Rather, they have been haphazardly excavated and their findings missing critical details. By now, we should be able to determine whether the Calusa and their neighbors were classic matriarchal or patriarchal lineal-descent societies or egalitarian, hierarchal, or a combination of both in terms of how they organized their leadership and social organization. From the notes of Cushing, Moore, and others, when researching Glade and Gladelike burials, there are indications that in South Florida, everyone deserved a good burial, suggesting a oneness and unity. The distinctive eight and nine separate burial mounds with causeways at Big Mound City and Big Circle Mound suggest the prominent role played by the kinship/clan. The total disregard for researching these important areas is a missing step that has set back pre-Columbian archaeology in South Florida by decades. Milanich was correct when pointing the finger at the lack of excavation. I assert that even more to blame is the way sites were excavated.

After my cross-cultural research, I contend that the Calusa were dominant because they gave more than they took. Their leaders were great and had longevity because of their generosity. Their leaders were great because of their skills with building strong and durable alliances. Equally, the Mayaimi people must have had strong leadership also, and together these groups achieved special status and importance as protectors of the sacred lake, as alliances managed prosperity and defense of coastal and interior resources and people. Both societies gained wealth derived from trade. It is not conjecture but common sense that societies that enjoyed such abundant natural resources combined with good leadership could afford the investment in large earthwork projects and a rich material culture compared with hand-to-mouth subsistence societies. In both groups their people bought into the different beliefs of each other, which resulted in a larger and regionally unifying belief system over time. I see examples of this in the Everglades region far south and as far north as Lake Kissimmee and the Tampa Bay region. As the years passed, every generation experienced shared interest and traditions, centuries of peace and plenty with the proper redistribution of wealth. By aligning themselves with the spiritual and religious center around Lake Okeechobee, the evolving beliefs brought unity of purpose, which resulted in many material and labor-intensive ceremonial complexes that further served as enduring visual symbols of unity for the inhabitants and all who traded and visited South Florida. Prior in South America thirty centuries before and in Louisiana twenty-two centuries before, other indigenous cultures achieved the same results using the same economic model, but with more reliance on a generous nation like the United States.

The recent anthropology of University of Florida graduate student Nathan Lawres demonstrates the need for new and varied models when approaching cultures that build many ceremonial mound complexes. He insists on including an ontological model in South Florida. This shift from entirely economic or environmental models has added greatly to research on Mississippi cultures. You would not take a study of Freemasons that excluded metaphysics and argued the movement entirely in economic terms.

The function of ritual complex does not exclude economics. World history is full of examples, beginning in the Neolithic period, of trade occurring at shrines and temples. If I learned one thing from anthropology, it is that when humans gather, economics is likewise to be present. There is every reason to believe, despite no research on the subject, that besides the lake region being a religious center, it was also an important trade hub. The Belle Glades ceramics attributed to the Lake People were found in great quantities over several periods all over the southern region. Add to that Sears's listing of excavated ceramic types from Fort Center to include ceramics from both the St. Johns region and Crystal River, and it is realized that a great deal more than ritual was happening in the region. Geography clearly shows that the fastest trade route from East to West coasts was across the lake by boat. Their predecessors at Poverty Point likewise built their monumental complex at a major trade hub. Like the kingdom of Mali in Africa, the Poverty Point people were involved in the salt trade to the center in the north.

I contend that there is a bigger picture that has gotten lost in the research after 1980. As I will discuss in the next chapter, there apparently was a rush to judgment by researchers attempting to interpret the culture regions and chronologies for South Florida. As a relatively new and undocumented area, the region was ripe for interpretation, often ignoring the previous record and literature. It was and remains very much a reinvention. One thing is clear: in the rush to author the new archaeology for the south, there exists many findings and assemblages that do not fit. Perhaps the most significant were the canal systems unique to the entire southern region, those and the other distinctively Calusa elements such as the pond feature and mounds at the mortuary complex. Then there was the Great Circle. Sears's own student, Robert Carr, documented eight other great circles from the Lake Kissimmee area to Dade County, Florida. In 1985 he specifically documented a circular ditch and embankments on the Caloosahatchee River (clearly the Calusa culture area) that had numerous ceremonial features, including a pond. The evidence of these ceremonial circles in the areas discovered by Carr alone not only disputes a theory excluding Calusa involvement but also contradicts Goggin's and subsequently Milanich's defined and distinct South Florida culture regions. These are examples of what I refer to as decades of disregard. For most of the post-1980 researchers, the Calusa was last week's flavor. But in order to create a narrative without the Calusa, pertinent data was simply disregarded. Anthropologists in the modern era demonstrate a field where attitude wins out over facts. In order to prove their point, they carefully pick and choose that which supports their view and discard or disregard all inconvenient facts.

In 2000, Ryan Wheeler self-published *Treasure of the Calusa*. His work displays the problem of highlighting the material culture of the Calusa in a post-Glade culture context. While Wheeler has been captivated by the art of the Calusa, he paints the picture of the Calusa as the recipients of the merging

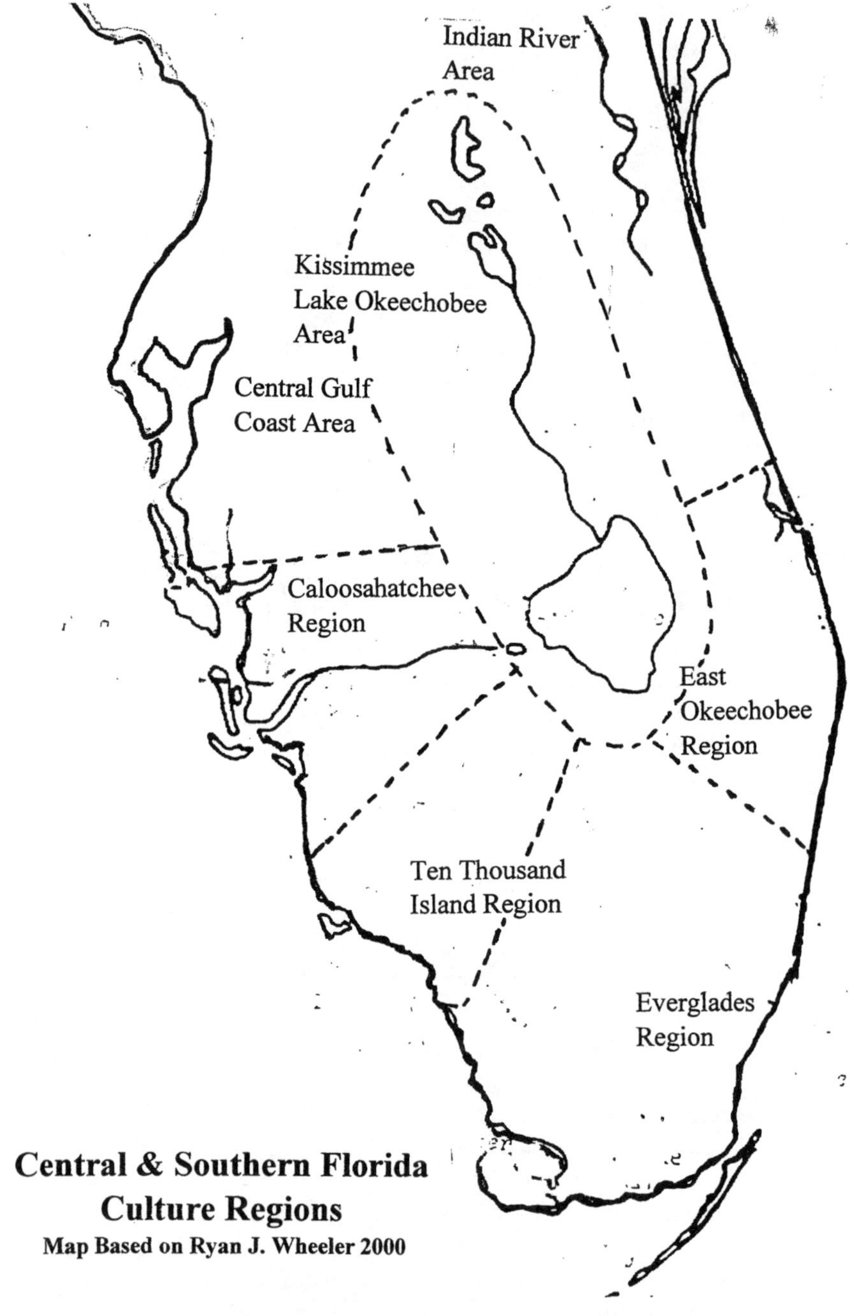

Figure 3.1. Map illustrating Wheeler's Glade Terminal Complex Area. Adapted from map that appears in *Treasure of the Calusa* (2000), self-published by Ryan J. Wheeler.

of beliefs and behaviors of the broader regional "Glade Terminal Complex." He not only speaks of the Glade Terminal Complex as a settled science when the literature shows that he was the first and only to use the construct, but he offers yet a third map and chronology for South Florida (figure 3.1). Wheeler, who was Florida's state archaeologist, returned to the concept of a single South Florida culture region, with many subcultural areas, but this time it is projected based more on beliefs, burials, and nonceramic artifacts. He didn't know what I discovered about the "Glade Region" not having clay. Wheeler's contributions by illustrating and researching artifacts after the European contacts are significant, but his insistence on a Glade Terminal Complex is premature and has no agreement or sufficient science. In chapter 9, I too will argue for a single South Florida culture region, but as the product of cultural synthesis and unequal contributions, not a slow merging with multiple and equal causes. I will in essence reinstate a long-held view in cultural anthropology of a culture region being defined by shared beliefs.

• 4 •

Culture Regions and Chronologies That Don't Work

I have attempted to show how recent archaeological investigations along the coast give the clues which enable us to incorporate the results of almost a century of earlier digging into such an overall reconstruction. This by no means implies that I pretend to have written the "final word."

—Gordon Willey, *Archaeology of the Florida Gulf Coast*

Perhaps most definitely, this research demonstrates the need for detailed radiocarbon profiles for sequences of site occupation at a greater number of sites across the Caloosahatchee region.

—Theresa Schober, "Deconstructing and Reconstructing Caloosahatchee Shell Mound Building"

Unlike neighboring states, by the 1940s Florida lacked a basic mapping of culture regions and their dates and chronologies. This was critical for anthropologists and archaeologists to correlate distinctive cultures to each other in a temporal setting within the Florida peninsula and to those in North America. Archaeology by the 1930s was employing more scientific methods for dating the various strata and artifacts as well. The scientific methodology coincided with an increase in archaeological excavations around the United States. Many as before were conducted by the Smithsonian and the federal government. The Great Depression, while terrible for so many, was good for large archaeological projects, and Florida was a major recipient. Between 1932 to 1937, a vast inventory of burial mounds and middens were excavated by teams working under the Civil Works Administration. In Florida, as always, the majority were conducted in North and Central Florida. In the south, however, the first prehistoric Everglades sites were excavated and their data retrieved.

The only other of note, and important to this book, was the excavation of the Belle Glade, Palm Beach County burial mound and midden in the Lake Okeechobee Basin. It would be the last time in Florida history that large-scale archaeology would be conducted.

By circumstances and not importance, this excavation led to the naming of all ceramics produced in the south, the term used to describe the entire culture region and the construct of a people and culture later to overshadow and compete with all of the Calusa accomplishments in the region. All of what I just recounted occurred in only thirty years, a record in archaeological time.

As a researcher and writer, you can deal with and recognize bias and predisposition. As a writer and researcher, you can resolve confusion and restore a culture's credibility. But when prior science has inadequately and unreliably established the places and times for your work, then your research just hangs out there in search of a place and time. As an author, I risk a great deal by including a chapter pertaining to dates. The number-one complaint by students regarding social studies is the learning of and memorizing of important dates. I will attempt to make this chapter as painless as possible. There is always the alternative of just trusting me and going to the next chapter. I would encourage the faint of heart to stay with the subject because like almost every date-based fact you were taught as a student pertaining to human evolution, prehistory, and the peopling of the New World were all wrong, or soon to be found wrong. The science and technology employed in archaeological dating has dramatically changed what we think we know about the past. Advances have made dating much more exacting and reliable. The difference with the past is so great that it has necessitated going back and researching all previous finds. A specific example related to my research here is in Thompson and Pluckhahn's redating of the Fort Center site and the work by William Sears. In the case of Fort Center and the Calusa, five hundred years makes a big difference. All researchers know that dates are not fixed. New excavations definitely show more reliable dating available. Typically, though, they work on the cheap and cannot afford sending things out to costly labs. All too often researchers rely on previous archaeology that lacked accurate dating. The sum total of their work then sufferers.

If you are an avid reader of all things prehistoric, then you already know. If you are not, here is what you can expect via the new, more accurate and reliable technologies. All previously documented dates are too recent, so add centuries or even millennium. Theories regarding the migration of people from the Old to the New World were incorrect. You cannot have folks living in the Amazon rain forest in 30,000 BC if they came over the Bering Strait land bridge from Asia in 14,000 BC. Correspondingly, if the oldest excavated human settlement in the Americas is in southern Chile and the more recent sites are in Alaska, what does that tell you? Growing up, I loved exploring the Olmecs, Mayans, and Aztecs. Now I enjoy the origins of a great deal of that right in the United States. Add to all of this the advances in DNA tracking and you have the perfect storm ready to topple our knowledge of the past. Jerald Milanich referred to such changes in his 1998 *Florida's Indians from Ancient Times to the Present* as a "trauma producing fact."

If there are two guiding principles related to archaeological dating I have learned after twenty-five years of research, it is: advances in technology has resulted in almost all dates upon new investigations are much older than previously believed. The older the dates, the new dating takes prior dating back many centuries. Using Florida as an example, redating after the 1980s resulted in early benchmarks being sent back an average of five hundred years—half a millennium. The second principle is that the closer the cultural period is to the present, the shorter the period is in duration. This is the current future shock theory, where because of technology, cultural change speeds up.

I wrote this chapter before the completion of my investigation into the existence of clays in South Florida. This chapter was written to challenge the archaeological spatial and temporal framework currently used in Florida. Since day one of archaeology in Florida, ceramics, the location of regional occurrences of ceramic "types," and their dating have formed the basis for the origins of Florida cultures, the geographical boundaries of the culture, and changes over time. By proving that twenty-one recognized southern Florida types and ten central Gulf Coastal types were not made locally, there now is the need to use other assemblages and cultural traits, not ceramic, to locate the culture and its changes over time.

Before moving on, I want to state that I am 100 percent confident in the results of my clay research. That the specific types of clays appropriate for ceramics do not exist in the areas I have studied is not a theory. It is a geological fact. Like gold or even iron, based on events and temperatures, an area either has the specific mineral resources or it does not (see figure 4.1).

The biggest obstacle in the past to accurate dating—and it is a major one—is the cost. Now the need to pull samples and do expensive testing of the clays for chemical and mineral components will come into play as well. In the absence of government-funded archaeology, researchers have been working on a shoestring. Often, they use their own funds. Today it cost around $600 to have one pottery sherd carbon dated by an approved lab. I have not found the costs associated with petrography. Almost all sites have varying dates of occupation and different strata. Dating then becomes too expensive. The work is then done without scientific dating. The existing chronologies in Florida reflect this consistent cutting of corners.

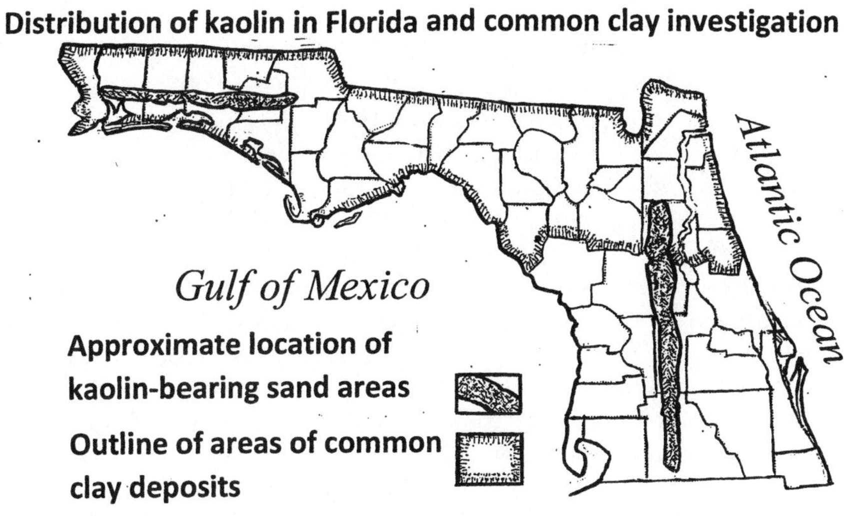

Figure 4.1. Map of Florida's clays and kaolin. Adapted from a map that appeared in a Florida Geological Survey of the clays and kaolin deposits. James Calver (1949).

Returning to my research on the Calusa in South Florida, because anthropologist have long established that they did not make ceramics, researchers have typically relied on other artifacts and their earthworks for a working chronology. With the change of the region to the Caloosahatchee cultural region, Glade ceramics have been established to determine Calusa chronology. This is a classic example of the resistance of researchers to go through ceramic withdrawal. Noted anthropologist Clarence B. Moore wrote in his Gulf Coast journal circa 1900 that he was dissatisfied with his excavations on burial mounds in the Calusa, which were due to the lack of pottery. He referred to ceramic artifacts as the "reward" for all archaeological research. Today, we know such little data on the Calusa for exactly the reason stated by Moore. Researchers perceive a lack of rewards for their efforts.

It just makes common sense. The story of exceptionalism that was the result of cultural synthesis by the Calusa and the Mayaimi, a twenty-five-century epoch, is in my view a story worth the research and scrutiny of details. Making the story even more important from the view of world history would be its relationship to the Poverty Point similar phenomena that started eight hundred years earlier and further north. Poverty Point, as well as the new theories of Martin Byers, could radically alter the anthropology of the Mayaimi and Calusa. The Fort Center site in Glade County, as well as the Aqui Esta mound and Big Mound Key mounds in Charlotte County, when revisited could result in a greater understanding of hunter-gathering societies and long-distance, complex organizational strategies connecting the Archaic period with the Woodland period. A strategy evolved to mitigate increased permanence and associated chiefdoms.

A link between Poverty Point to Fort Center in Florida during the twentieth century would have been impossible working with any of the three existing sequences and chronologies. When Thompson and Pluckhahn got earlier dates for the Great Circle and the mound/pond mortuary complex, it brought the start dates for the Great Circle to BC 800 to 690, a time when Poverty Point was still in progress and being used as an immense regional ritual center. As I have stated, I strongly disagree with not only Sears's theory of the function of the Great Circle, but also his insistence on the Calusa playing no role in its construction of the mortuary mound complex there. I insist that the many carved wooden effigies were definitively Calusa. Thompson and Pluckhahn redated not only the mound/pond mortuary complex but also tests were done on the wooden effigies. New dates for the mound/pond complex are AD 80 to 650 and AD 180 to 340. Dates for the wooden animal and bird effigies came in at AD 540 to 650. Notice how precise the new technology is getting dating down to just a few decades. Without really any reliable dating for Calusa sites, it has been approximated that the Calusa were here around 500 BC. Therefore, time chronologies used by Sears and others can no longer be used to disqualify the Calusa from the Fort Center complex because of dates.

The simple but profound redating of Fort Center in 2012 will have a significant effect on previous theory and conclusions. William Sears used Fort Center to create an entirely new Belle Glades centrist view of the entire South Florida region. He signaled a divorce from the predominant view expressed in 1964 by Goggin and Sturtevant of a Calusa-centered view. Sears broke with all before him by creating a new version of Goggin's single Glade culture region and chronology by replacing it with an Okeechobee-centered Glade region and corresponding chronology. It was radical in that Sears used his manipulated data from a single site to replace the research of dozens of archaeologists spanning one hundred years.

My extensive research of the literature reveals that Sears casually put the Belle Glade centrist view into the research in a 1964 article in the *Florida Anthropologist.* In remarks at the conclusion of the article and prefaced with "this is not the place," Sears wrote regarding the Calusa sites visited:

> Most of them have some evidence for contact upstream with the Lake Okeechobee Basin in the form of Belle Glade sherds which are the characteristic pottery of the Belle Glade culture area.

This one and only affirmation of a "Belle Glade culture" was subsequently jumped on by Jerald Milanich, who used it as the basis for the existence of the "Belle Glade" culture in his two books in the 1990s. Despite that there was no empirical evidence for a "Belle Glade" people and culture, now it was in the literature. The rest is history. The irony is that Sears's article was about the Calusa sites in Cape Coral, Lee County, Florida. His remarks were meant to endorse a Caloosahatchee subregion of the existing single Glade culture region and not a Belle Glade culture region. We know this because in his 213-page book on Fort Center, he makes no reference to a Belle Glade culture or people.

If you were to take one agreed-upon period in South Florida prehistory that was the most important and dynamic after 1982, all would agree it was the Glade II period. Sears stated that using Fort Center and his dating that the Glade II period began in 200 AD and lasted until 600 to 800 AD, four to six centuries. Sears stated that during that period the Okeechobee culture was intensely focused on the construction of the ritual center at Fort Center to the exclusion of all else. Despite the authority being Goggin, who formulated his theory based on the evidence that Glades II began in 25 BC and ended 400 AD, truth be told Sears needed the four hundred years to create a nonexistent village with intensive agriculture. As I will discuss later, Milanich authored new culture regions and periods to replace Goggin's. To accommodate Sears's work, one of the new culture regions in Florida prehistory he classified as "Okeechobee." Milanich did not provide time periods, therefore leaving Sears's Glades I–IV as the periods and dates for the Okeechobee culture region. The single redating in 2012 had to have been "trauma producing." The researchers still rely primarily on ceramics to determine and fix dates for all the Florida culture periods. The new dates for Fort Center indicate that the ceramic periods are off in South Florida by as much as four centuries. This is why, despite the urge, most of the theoretical changes to the regions and periods in South Florida have been seriously premature. Now that it is a fact that all Glade ceramics, regardless of dating, were exported to the area and not locally produced, not only were the findings premature, they were seriously flawed and based solely on assumption and not scientific fact.

The prehistoric regional cultures did not develop in a vacuum. When you change one culture or one period, it affects all the others. Again, since most ceramics had been dated back in the 1930s and possibly inaccurately, they are not reliable for newer site summaries. A continuously changing Florida culture and region has been the Weeden Island culture. Weeden Island, a specific site in St. Petersburg, Florida, in the Great Tampa Bay, very early defined an essentially northern Florida culture. Since the 1990s, Florida anthropologists believe that the Weeden Island culture morphed into the Safety Harbor culture in the central Gulf Coast region of Florida, previously the lower region of the Weeden Island group. As a result of my findings, all ceramics were exported to this region. There are two possible accessible sources for ceramics, both out of their regions. Elemental analysis would show if one or both areas were the sources for all of the Weeden and Safety Harbor ceramic types. Fortunately, unlike the Glade region, anthropologists have fully researched the other facets that defined these groups as distinctive cultures.

Goggin's Florida regions and chronologies (figure 4.2) were published the same year as Willey's. Goggin did not agree with Willey and believed even in 1949 that the dates for many periods were much earlier. Willey published his four-plus-century-long Glade II period at AD 800 to 1250. Therefore, when Sears published his Glades II dates in 1982, there was a difference of 750 years between the two schools. This underscores the importance of dating and redating. As it turns out, Goggin was correct and not Sears due to the 2013 dates at Fort Center. Even without the knowledge of no physical clay in regions, there have been no attempts to reconcile this critical discrepancy. This is why the new graduates end up pulling their hair out. The regions and periods simply don't work.

Imagine if you will that researchers traveled to the various sites with canals all over South Florida and gathered dates using the new technologies. Who would win? The Belle Glades centrists or the Calusa centrists or both? What would the excavations and dating of Big Mound City and Big Circle Mound reveal about the last seven centuries before 1700 in South Florida? At the present rate and the fact that the majority of such sites have been destroyed, we will probably never know the answers. Florida's best-kept secrets will remain just that, secrets.

A fact that has created problems for developing a compete Florida taxonomy was that Willey had no excavations below Punta Gorda in Charlotte County except the 1937 Gene Stirling and Lloyd Reichard work in Palm Beach County, so his work was incomplete. This was because with the exception of Cushing in 1896 and Moore, there was no data to use. Goggin spent three years in South Florida in order to provide more data for the Glade period and chronology. Even today, however, the lack of excavation data is still insufficient when compared to the central and northern Florida regions.

Willey clearly concluded that based on the archaeology of the Tampa Bay region, that a separate culture and chronology existed during the transition period from the Archaic to the Early Woodland. Ceramics indicate that a primarily Gulf Coast culture, the Deptford and its later manifestations, Swift Creek and Santa Rosa, stopped on the northern edge of Tampa Bay. The people south of there made very plain, sand-tempered ceramics. Willey via Goggin stated that this culture was characteristic of the southern Glades people. This was supported by the archaeology of many sites in Hillsborough, Manatee, Sarasota, and Charlotte counties. Choosing one site, Willey and Goggin

	Northwest Gulf Coast	Central Gulf Coast	Glades Area	Indian River Area	Northern St.Johns	Central Florida
1700	Seminole	Seminole	Seminole	Seminole	Seminole	Seminole
1600	Late Jefferson	Safety	Glades IIIC	St. Augustine	St. Augustine St. Johns	Potazo
1500	Fort Walton	Harbor	Glades IIIB		IIC	Alachua
1400				Malabar III	St. Johns IIB	
1300	Weeden Island II	Weeden Island II	Glades IIIA		St. John IIA	Hickory Pond
1200						
1100	Weeden Island I	Weeden Island I	Glades IIC			Cades Pond
1000						
900						
800			Glades IIB			
700				Malabar II	St. Johns I Late	
600						
500						
400	Santa Rosa Swift Creek					Pre Cades Pond
300			Glades IIA		St. Johns Early	
200						
100		Perrico Island				
-0-						
100				Malabar I		
200	Deptford		Glades			
300						
400						
500						
600						
700						
800	Orange ?	Orange?		Orange	Orange	Orange
1500	PreCeramic		PreGlades			Preceramic
1800		Suwanee Points?		Mt. Taylor	Mt. Taylor	Suwanee Points?

Figure 4.2. Chart showing culture regions and their chronologies. Note Goggin's attention to slight changes in South Florida Glades ceramics, his area of interest. Adapted from John Goggin's chart first published in the *Florida Anthropologist* (1950).

referred to this culture as Perico Island. It was clear to see that they were not part of the culturally distinctive Deptford or the Weeden Island cultures. The region had the same Belle Glades and Glade ceramics found in the Calusa sites, the Lake Okeechobee sites, and clear down to the tip of the peninsula. So, the region, a small fraction of the size of the south and the northern cultures—about five thousand square miles—was designated a Gladelike northern region of the predominant southern Glades cult. Not one researcher since has begged to question if the Perico was actually part of the Glade culture and chronology. The same year Sears published *Fort Center*, researchers Luer and Almy renamed the culture and assigned dates but kept it as a separate culture and period. Their culture chronology created gaps of several centuries. Their research never related their views with the Glade or the Calusa archaeology. Their work did what Sears's had done—Luer and Almy created the Manasota culture, periods, and people. Not so much the site caused the shift, but rather the pronouncement by archaeologist Ripley Bullen that Perico ceramics were found much further north in Citrus and Pasco counties. First, this particular limestone-tempered pottery is very rare. There are indications that it probably never originated at the Perico sites. Willey and Goggin never based the Perico culture and period on anything but the "southern" Belle Glade and Glade ceramics common to that region. But again, big fish, small pond, new Manasota culture, new period, and definitely not Calusa. The region, the data, as before had not changed, just the perceptions of the researchers. A minute detail by a respected researcher caused a reshuffling of the regions and periods. I mention this because it is an example of how one change impacts the taxonomies and chronologies of other regions. Their research, I believe, is also an example of prematurity. Like the Calusa, Luer and Almy concluded that the Manasota culture did not produce their ceramics. You can research all the ceramic collections stored at the Florida Museum of Natural History and never find a "Manasota ceramic" vessel. You will find multiple examples of Byers's Hopewellian model in play. Ceramics, other than everyday types, were all associated with burials. I contend that the Manasota and their neighbors were far less settled as believed. More than likely they were uncharacteristically more transient fishing-hunter-gatherers way into the Woodland period. Ceramics did not travel well, which would account for their absence, except at mortuary/burial sites or middens associated with transregional feasting and ceremonies.

Ceramics did not travel well, but baskets did. Florida's environment is ill suited for basket artifacts surviving over time. We know from the Windover Pond water burials that Paleo-Indians were excellent weavers of native fibers. When researching the clay situation in Florida, USGS surveys of the upper Great Plains also came up as minus clays. History shows the indigenous people were dedicated nomads. History also shows their rich basket-making skills. Logically, the mound-building societies of prehistoric Florida hauled great quantities of shells and sand. Basketry and not pottery would define such societies.

So far, I have shown John Goggin's work on regions and chronologies to be superior when new dating is performed. At the same time Sears published his Okeechobee-centered Glades periods, Jerald Milanich and William Sturtevant completely revised Willey's and Goggin's regions and chronologies (figure 4.3). Implied but not stated, Milanich also wished to reflect Sears's work at Fort Center by changing the established view of a single southern Glade culture region to add a separate region for the monumental earthworks around Lake Okeechobee. Together with Charles Fairbanks, they published the revision to Goggin's South Florida taxonomy in 1980. Milanich recounts in his 1994 book:

> It was becoming obvious that south Florida was not a single-culture region. A revised taxonomy was needed that expanded Goggin's concept of a single Glades culture for south Florida. Variations in archaeological assemblages existed among geographical areas, as well as through time, suggesting that cultural regions could be defined within south Florida.

What resulted were the Glades, Okeechobee, and Caloosahatchee (Calusa) culture regions. The south now had three separate and distinct culture regions. Milanich charted them and assigned the periods and dates except for Okeechobee in *Archaeology of Precolumbian Florida* (1994). One can assume that Sears's Fort Center periods and chronologies would be used for the new Okeechobee culture region. There were no significant excavations and findings at Calusa or Glades sites to warrant their inclusion in the new systems. Likewise, Sears's Fort Center was the only significant excavation in South Florida at the time.

Likewise, Milanich seemed that he wanted to accommodate Ripley Bullen, George Luer, and Marion Almy by changing also the Perico Island culture and chronology, even though no new assemblages were discovered. It is apparent from the history that from 1980 forward, anything that dispelled the belief that South Florida was a single Glade culture was a good thing and represented informed and progressive archaeology. Likewise, any research that would reduce the scope, influence, and significance of the Calusa was a step in the right direction. The University of Florida with the Florida Museum of Natural History had successively eradicated cultural ethnographic research models, replacing them with progressive "historical-ecology" models. It was the environment and not the people.

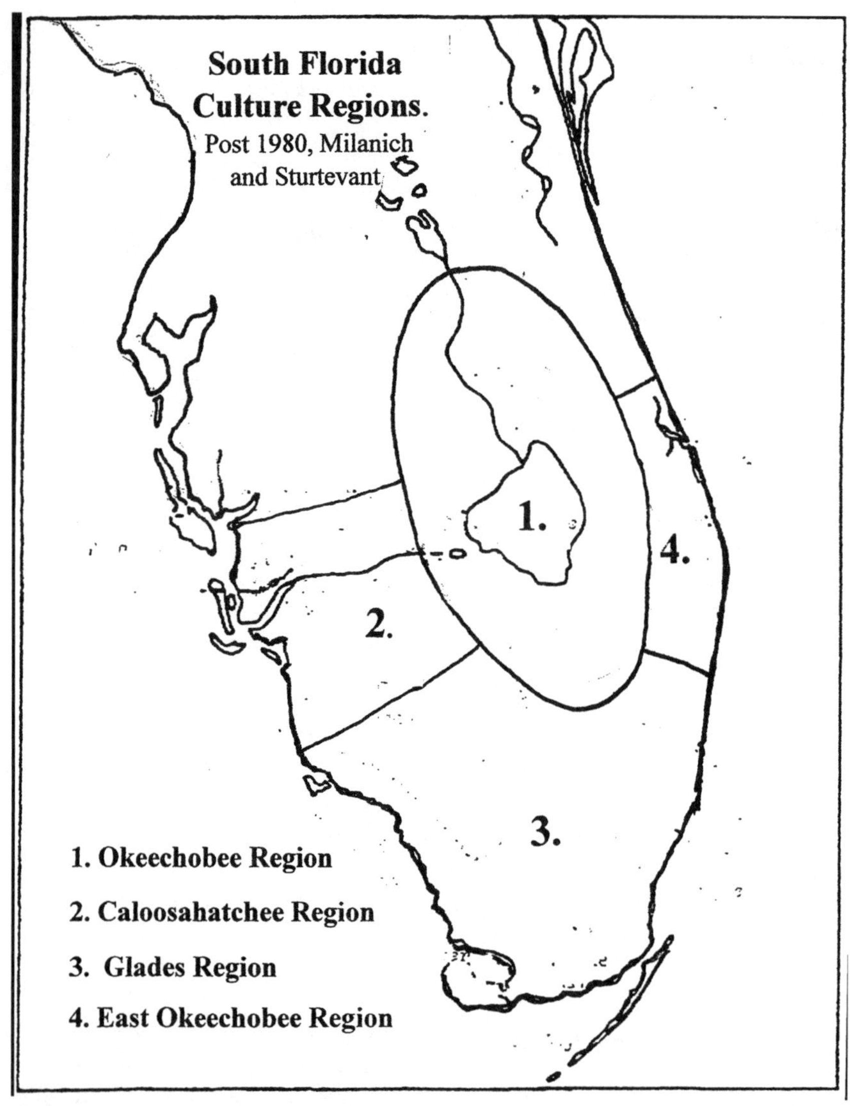

Figure 4.3. Map showing the Milanich and Sturtevant post-1980 culture regions of South Florida. Adapted from a Jerald Milanich chart published in *Archaeology of Pre-Columbian Florida* (1994), The University of Florida Press.

On the same page, Milanich stated that his new nomenclature and chronologies were "not entirely satisfactory," claiming a problem correlating the postcolonial Calusa and Tequesta to their regions prior to the Europeans was difficult. In simple language, he hoped that it was proven that prior to the arrival of the Europeans it would be shown that the Belle Glades people he invented would be the dominant cultural force in South Florida. Wait until he has to try to disprove my findings on the ceramics that form the basis for all cultures and periods.

The same problem, but not mentioned by Milanich, was the postcolonial Calusa and the Manasota (formerly Perico) to their regions prior to the Europeans. This problem worsened when Milanich encouraged one of his graduate students to write a paper proving that it wasn't either the Perico or the Manasota, but rather the Safety Harbor culture who were the heirs to the northern portion of the South Florida region, a premise that drove a six-hundred-year wedge in the period's chronologies. The student reviewed all of the findings from the Perico Island period sites for the presence of Safety Harbor ceramics, a much later culture and culture period. Based on a very few findings of Safety Harbor–style ceramics, he forced the research to prove a longer and more influential Safety Harbor period in the Glades and Calusa culture region. The student, Jeffrey Mitchem, the same student who had written the excellent burial mound paper, authored a four-time period sequence for Safety Harbor. Based on the principles I outlined earlier, the Safety Harbor dates are much ado about nothing. Most archaeologists have the Safety Harbor culture, based on the ceramics at 1425 AD. Therefore, the entire Englewood and Pinellas periods are suspect. The Tatham, considering the lack of proper dating being a sixty-seven-year-long period, is ridiculous. Then employing both geography and common sense, Englewood, which was a single site excavated during the early archaeological age, was closer to the Calusa towns that were prominent on the coast during that period by many miles compared with the distance between Englewood and Safety Harbor. Englewood was only ninety miles west of the Fort Center ritual complex. Finally, it's a historical fact that the Calusa gained in power and influence by 1500. How could a chiefdom five thousand square miles at its zenith have more cultural influence than the Calusa/Glades culture that encompassed over fifteen thousand square miles? Some narratives are difficult to embrace.

Returning to my preference for the relevance and applicability of Byers's models, everything about the Englewood burial mound looks like an example of a site that was built and maintained jointly by an autonomous local community and an autonomous transient cult group who were jointly responsible for the site. The reemergence of the stabilizing social organizing strategy, Byers sets at 200 BC the start date for the Hopewell culture. When you consider that the sixteen-mound ceremonial complex, with the mortuary/burial complex at Fort Center, started as early as 800 BC, just as mound-building in Florida proceeded those in Ohio, Florida hunter-gatherers played a significant role in this reemerging social system variation. This would also explain why so many researchers suggest a strong connection between the Safety Harbor culture and the Hopewell-Mississippian cultures. Remember also, Willey's dates for Englewood and all others have been proven to be off by one thousand years. This would put the Englewood complex at 100 BC. The neighboring Perico Island complex Willey had tentatively set at 650 AD, take away one thousand years, and the site probably dates at 350 BC.

I am indebted to anthropologist George Luer, who brought to my attention two Calusa sites close to my home that have Poverty Point similarities: Big Mound Key, a thirty-seven-acre site on Charlotte Harbor dated 850 BC; and across Turtle Bay, the John Quiet Mound complex. Both have the semicircular ridges only found at Poverty Point (figure 2.1). True to the Calusa style, the John Quiet site has a hand-dug canal leading to the central mound from the bay. These sites not only provide evidence for a Calusa/Poverty Point connection, but they also contradict any theory of a non-Calusa influence in the northern areas. The fact also that Big Mound Key has four burial mounds, uncommon in Florida, could indicate a jointly affiliated complex, as discussed by Byers.

The changes in culture when viewing prehistoric hunter-gathering societies have been few over time. In the case of those whose changes were extraordinary, they were still few but quite dramatic. When Gordon Willey published his complete taxonomy with chronology for all the culture regions in Florida, the eight-hundred-page unbiased synopsis was correlated to the two major connecting regions, Georgia and the Lower Mississippi. Goggin in turn became a dedicated specialist, a big fish in a small pond to mirror both Fox and Granberry. Like Milanich thirty years later, Goggin was so involved in Glades archaeology that what would be considered as a minor change when compared with Central or North Florida, let alone Georgia and the Lower Mississippi regions, became classified as a separate and distinctive culture period. This is shown in his Glade II a, b, and c micro periods, and his Glade III, a, b, and c periods. We see this mistake repeated with Milanich at the helm. Milanich created a Glades II a, b, and c, as well as a Glades II a and b. For his Caloosahatchee periods, he created a Caloosahatchee a and b, as well as a separate Caloosahatchee IV, a two-century-long period of questionable need. Why I say the new taxonomy and accompanying chronologies don't work is they do not correlate with Central and North Florida and the connecting culture regions. The mishaps due to the premature changes to the southern regions and periods in a fifty-year period has caused so much uncertainty, so many contradictions, that the next generation of researchers will be severely handicapped.

The year is 2000, the beginning of a new millennium, and Ryan Wheeler self-publishes what he believes to be the final and complete taxonomy for culture regions in South Florida. True to the excesses of the liberal academic mindset, Wheeler's regions, without chronologies, were inclusive of all cultures. In an age where there are no losers and everyone gets a trophy for participation, Wheeler determined in a book supposedly about the Calusa artifacts that South Florida had five separate and distinct culture regions: Kissimmee Lake Okeechobee Region, East Okeechobee Region, Everglades Region, Ten Thousand Island Region, and Caloosahatchee Region. Seriously, the Tequesta were major cultural players in the coastal portions of the East Okeechobee region and the Everglades. The Calusa were a major player in the Ten Thousand Island Region, and soon, it will be an archaeological fact that the Kissimmee River Valley was a part of the Lake Okeechobee Region. Wheeler again creates a problem.

During my intensive research in preparation for this book, I have tried to find the big picture, knowing that the public does not share the intense preoccupation with minute details that are the hallmark of specialism in a single culture or period. At some point, dates and culture sequences are extremely important. Without proper dating, you cannot realize the big picture and the pieces will never fit. As I pointed out in my preface, searching for relationships is critical for success. Often you must find those connecting pieces in another seemingly unrelated piece of research. As a lay person, I can assure you that the researchers guard their precious information. Many will not return your emails, letters, or calls requesting information. Those researchers who respond are cautious, protective, and very measured in their responses. All of the specialists have stated that they give one kind of answer to lay people and the public versus one of their own. That goes for quantitative answers such as dates. This chapter, this book is probably the first attempt to deal meaningfully with a prehistory culture taxonomy and chronology since Willey's and Goggin's sixty-nine years ago in order to share this knowledge with the public. I am sure that my theories are the first interdisciplinary-driven theories. For me, it is common sense that the cultural environment, increased populations, and warfare affected culture periods and chronologies as much as changes in the physical environment. When I found George Milner's 2014 extensive research on periods of warfare and periods of peace, trends defined critical culture periods in the southeastern portion of North America and my research of the Calusa and Mayaimi in South Florida.

Milner's cross-cultural archaeological evidence shows a period of marked increases in violence and warfare from 3000 BC to 100 BC. This period is followed by a brief period of peace from 100 BC to AD 400 (note that Byers's reemergence starts at 200 BC). All trade and the possibility for permanent settlements and resulting investments in building mounds and ceremonial earthworks would be affected by either war or peace. Also, the change to permanent settlements after thousands of years of nomadic life would not be welcomed by many. Until Thompson and Pluckhahn returned and redated the earth constructions at Fort Center, those achievements did not fit with others in the Southeast. Now they do, and as such should drive an entirely new period of research. Using Thompson and Pluckhahn and not Sears, Goggin, or Milanich, the mortuary complex, mounds, pond, and effigies, now considered the most significant hunter-gatherer–built earthworks in the world (Thompson and Pluckhahn 2014), were built at a time of peace. During the same five-hundred-year period the area witnessed Weeden Island I, Swift Creek in central to northwest Florida and Marksville in Louisiana in the Lower Mississippi region, and Hopewell in the Ohio River Valley. That the start of the Marksville culture, being Tunica, the ancestors of the Calusa as well as the first appearance of the Hopewell culture in the Deep South, makes this prehistoric epoch quite remarkable. Large projects involving burial mounds were a common feature. Freedom to trade without fear of attack is underscored by the ceramics found from Fort Center in South Florida up to Perico Island in Bradenton to Crystal Rivers in Pasco County to Swift Creek in northern Florida up to Marksville in the Mississippi River Valley.

I even found confirmation of this peaceful period and corresponding cultural achievements on page 217 of Milanich's *Archaeology of Precolumbian Florida*. While discussing the Weeden Island period, Milanich found great similarities between the River Styx Mound complex, Crystal River, and Cross Creek mound complexes further north with the mortuary mound complex at Fort Center. All of those were dated at 100 to 300 AD. Besides their more monumental scale and horseshoe-shaped embankments, each site had an abundance of trade goods. I liken it to expansion and contraction. Cultures expand, move out from the center, share, and trade when there is less chance of violence.

This has caused me to rethink a great deal of the prehistory of North America. Archaeologists have done a great deal of research on the Hopewell culture. In Florida as I have discussed, researchers like Sears and Milanich see much of what they refer to as Hopewell cultural diffusion into Florida, even the Lake Okeechobee area. What they see are mounds and metal artifacts. If I am right about applying Martin Byers's research to Florida, it was the dual complementary autonomous ownership of these complexes, the extended kinships that mitigated the absolute authority of the chiefs that was the Hopewell connection. Researchers assign the dates of 200 AD to 600 AD to the entire Hopewell culture period. They also claim they cannot find an explanation for the "sudden disappearance of the culture that engineered the great Serpent Mound" (figure 6.1A). First, four centuries are not very long for a culture. Byers reassures us that Hopewell became the Mississippi culture. Just as in Florida, Weeden became Safety Harbor.

The violent period prior resulted in three major cultural achievements during a time when cultures were more insular, worked regionally, and did not risk long-distance trade and interactions. First was the building of shell ring regional ritual spaces with middens. Second was the making and perfecting of local and regional ceramic traditions in the northeast and northwest where clays where abundant, and finally the first large, circular earthen ditches in South Central Florida for regional rituals. Correspondingly, the archaeology shows that certain burial mounds and mortuary complexes were transregional and that based on widely dispersed cults and clanlike affiliated members, out-of-region members traveled with the deceased and their grave goods, thus mitigating local and interregional tensions and disputes (a strictly hunter-gatherer carryover at a time of permanent settlements and the increasing power of chiefdom).

My research of Fort Center proves that the mortuary complex at the site was attacked, burned, and desecrated around 800 AD (Ehmann 2018). Sears stated that the complex ceased to be used after that date. Milner proves that that date marked another increase in violence and warfare that lasted for seven hundred years. When the new age of violence emerged in the Southeast, there were far less hunter-gathering cultures. Most societies were agriculturalists or mixed economies. That is one big reason for my continued interest in the Calusa and their neighbors. The largest prehistoric civilization was the Mississippi culture from 800 AD to 1600. As an immense region, the culture lasted eight hundred prosperous and violent continuous centuries, one-third of the duration of the hunter-gathering culture in South Florida. Longevity belonged to hunter-gathering cultures. That is what a proper and redated chronology will show. Ceramics define only one-third of all the Florida culture regions, while all Florida cultures were invested in earthworks; that is, they were all mound-builders. A proper taxonomy and chronology should reflect not only that separation over time—hunter-gatherer, mixed, and complex—as well as show their developments from the Archaic period through to the Historic period or Post-Contact period.

The cultural events and their dates, Granberry's linguistic study, along with Gibson and Clark's Poverty Point research, along with Byers's complementary autonomous organization strategies (all Florida outsiders), helped me to formulate a new taxonomy and chronology. I believe the Great Circles and their new dating should guide the development of the new chart. The investment of these belief-driven earthwork constructions marked the beginning of a distinctive South Florida culture around 800 BC. This was not an isolated event. The date, monumentalism in construction, along with the linguistic connection, ties Fort Center to Poverty Point. By 200 BC, the war-torn region in the Lower Mississippi River culture region prompted a diaspora of

Tunica people, some migrating to southern Florida. I believe also that these people built canals, and they brought that engineering skill along with their kinship groups and religion to Florida.

The ceramic periods and culture regions for North Florida work. They are logically, by geography, linked to the greater Southeast region, as demonstrated by the early Deptford ceramic culture. I do believe, however, that presently the dating for those periods is off. Common sense would dictate that if ceramics began in Georgia in 1500 BC, such a technological advancement would be highly desirable and not take one thousand years to reach northern Florida, because, based on my findings that make it impossible to use ceramics as regional and chronologic benchmarks, my taxonomy utilizes social orga-

	Mississippi River	Georgia	N. Central Florida	St. Johns River	N. Western Florida	W. Central Florida	South Florida
1700 A.D. 1450	Mississippi c	Etowah Alachua c	St. Johns Alachua c	St. Johns ii m	Pensacola c	Safety Harbor m	South Florida hg
1200	Chahokia c	Okmulgee Etowah c	Weeden Island II m	St. Johns II m?	Weeden Island II Ft. Walton c	Safety Harbor m	South Florida hg
800 100 A.D.	Mississippi c	Kolomocki c	Weeden Island I m	St. Johns II hg	Alachua m	Deptford II Swift Creek m	South Florida hg
-0- 100 B.C. 800	Marksville hg	Deptford hg	St. Johns I hg	Deptford hg	Deptford hg	Deptford hg	South Florida hg
1500 B.C. B. C.	Poverty Point	Stallings Island hg	Orange hg	Orange hg	Deptford hg	Deptford hg	South Florida hg

C Complex/ Agriculture m Mixed, Agriculture & Hunter- Gathering hg Hunter-Gathering Only

Figure 4.4. Chart showing author's concept of a more simplified and relevant view of culture regions and their chronologies. The chart emphasizes sociopolitical organization and deemphasizes ceramics because all southern ceramics were the result of trade. Ted Ehmann, 2018.

nizing as the determinant. The chronology I propose would look something like the chart illustration, with hg = hunter-gatherers, m = mixed, and c = complex or chiefdom.

My proposed taxonomy and chronology (figure 4.4) are even more simplified than Willey's in that it eliminates three of Willey's and Goggin's cultural regions, Malabar, Perico Island, and Safety Harbor culture areas having origins and elements of two other more prominent culture regions. This is based on my research showing that Perico and its replacement the Manasota, and later Safety Harbor, were all definitively West Central Florida. In chapter 8, I will go into more detail. I believe that there has always been the tendency both to misinterpret culture regions due to trade ceramics and to create both new regions or an abundance of periods based on new and isolated discoveries. The revised dates have been long overdue. The new chart deals with major cultural changes and broad sweeps, free of ceramics to level the "playing field," which will allow new and graduating researchers to fit their research into an appropriate context without fear of errors and the expense of carbon dating ceramics in order to prove a compelling argument.

• 5 •

Humanizing Models for Understanding Adaptation

It is not important to know. It is only important to believe.

—Jean Cocteau

But clueless or not, I am disinclined to invest Archaic leaders with the ability to pull off such feats—feats—yes feats like building mounds, no. Why? Primarily because I have serious doubts about how successful Archaic leaders would have been at making people do something they did not want to do.

—Jon L. Gibson, *Signs of Power: The Rise of Cultural Complexity in the Southeast*

It is scarcely surprising that reasonable systems fail because people behave unreasonably.

—Robin Fox, *The Challenge of Anthropology*

In 1980 I enrolled in a two-year intensive study in Neuro-Linguistic Programing. Considered by its authors as a technology that mapped the subconscious mind, a major contributor was Robert Dilts. Dilts's research and practice in beliefs and beliefs systems was revolutionary. Later, this knowledge, combined with my study of bio-grammar, have provided me with a unique view in anthropological research. The human brain, like any other component of our biological and cultural system, is organized into levels. The brain has different logical levels of thinking and being (figure 5.1). There appears to be five levels that the human species and our cultures work with consistently. The basic or foundation level (the only or most important) as viewed by the archaeologists previously discussed is the environment that is characterized as external forces and restraints. Dilts calls this the "where" and "when." Using the

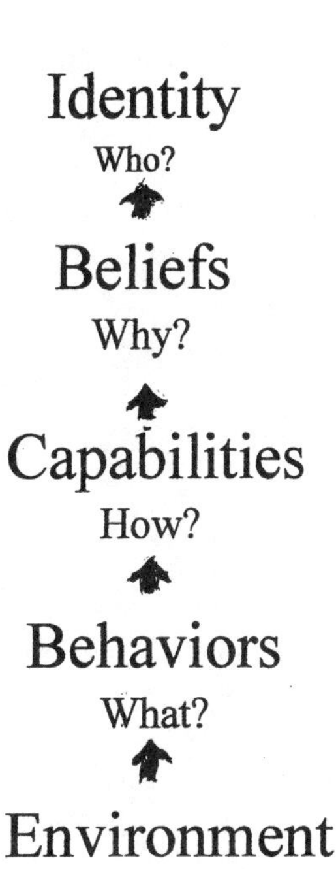

Figure 5.1. Chart of logical levels of organization in systems. Original chart in *Changing Belief Systems with NLP,* Robert Dilts (1990), Meta Publications.

Calusa, the where were the coastal regions. The second level is behaviors, the "what." Behaviors are what we do when interacting with the environment. With regard to their behaviors, they were fishing-hunter-gathering. It was also all their particular sociopolitical behaviors. Level three is your capabilities, the "how." All behavior is guided by prethought and hindsight, mental mapping, and trial and error. For the subject of the Calusa, it may have appeared as establishing power or influence by building strong regional alliances, perhaps building a system of canals or sponsoring religious sites and ceremonial mound projects. So far, I am in chartered waters. The above-mentioned organizational levels appear everywhere in anthropology and archaeology. The next two levels that clearly exist in our natural human systems are very uncomfortable areas for social scientists. Level four, the "why" level according to Dilts, is the level of beliefs and values. Capabilities are organized by beliefs and systems of beliefs. Level five, Identity, the who, organizes the beliefs. Beliefs challenge social scientists because they are not logical, nor are they factual; they are not "reasonable," nor do they have to be in order to work. No anthropologist understands this reality more than Robin Fox. Considering that human beliefs have survived to this day, there is more than ample proof that they are necessary, were selected for, and still are critical for human adaptation and survival.

Because of the nature of beliefs and that they exist on the subconscious level, they are, no matter how false or destructive, impossible to change. Another distinctive feature of beliefs is that they are not fragmentary. Ultimately with individuals and groups, beliefs organize into complete systems. I always use my growing up as an example. As a child I was short and chubby. When children were choosing teams for a sport activity, no one wanted to choose me. Belief one: I am no athlete. With little time in the sport soon came belief two: I am no good at sports. Not wishing to feel bad about my lack of capabilities and my inferiority as a male, belief number 3: sports are stupid. By the time I got to high school and was taller and had a better build, I declared that I hated sports.

Returning to the subject at hand, let us say you are a member of an established, functioning, and settled tribe of hunter-gatherers living by the tropical coastal waters in southwest Florida around 800 AD, and gradually your way of life and that of your group dramatically changes from rising sea levels (level one: your environment) and you are dealing with external pressures. It stands to reason that these changes will cause you to change your behaviors. If you do not change your behaviors, you and your people risk starving to death. The next steps or levels of organization are where we see incredible variation. Remember that according to Dilts beliefs are what organize the strategies required. In my example, it is reduced coastal food sources. Culture provides the memory needed to deal with any change or emergency. For the Calusa and Glade people, the cultural memory was stored in the myths, stories, and beliefs. Those key components of the cultural memory lived in and were recreated by the spiritual/religious leaders.

The environmentalists are correct in claiming that environment gives rise to the culture, but what results is only a basic outline. The individual features result from the trial and errors of selected behaviors. If they are deemed capable, then they get organized and structured into beliefs. Given all of this, which I believe is true about all humans and all cultures, you can understand why Sears's work at Fort Center was the way it was. Beliefs organized his approach. Beliefs brought all information into final agreement, even when it obviously was contrary to his beliefs in reality.

Returning to the Calusa, all strategies will need to be compatible with your beliefs. You can work with your religious leaders to communicate with the gods and the spirits as to your course of action, you can organize rituals to appeal to the gods to lower the sea levels, you can give up your power to a single person who will take control of the problem and organize relief efforts, you can change your way of life and develop other sources of food, you can organize raiding parties inland and steal their food, or you can conquer them and force them to supply you with food. This is why history is the story of human variations. Cultural evolutionists have never been comfortable with the persistence of egalitarian hunter-gathering societies of neighboring "civilizations" centuries into the Modern period. The lesson of the Calusa and Mayaimi people is precisely that belief systems differ from group to group. While like any component of cultural adaptation, beliefs are a response to environment, but how societies successfully adapt is organized entirely by beliefs, the subconscious organizing of the conscious, the intangible organizing the tangible. The more we understand this aspect of the natural human system, the less surprised and likely to reject what is observable in these ancient cultures.

In 2004, Poverty Point archaeologist Jon L. Gibson started the shift away from environmental determinism views of mound-building societies in North America toward a view that included beliefs. In a paper titled "The Power of Beneficent Obligation in First Mound-Building Societies," Gibson wrote:

> In my view, the real power behind first mound-building came out of the group mind. The power of which I speak undergirded practice and custom. It not only touched the core of Archaic society, it was the core. I am talking about those beliefs and attitudes that made people who they were and fired their deepest passions—those notions and feelings fated to bring action, communalistic action, and those that can transform individuals into single-minded social dynamics. I am talking about the power of beneficent obligation or debt of gratitude.

The recent work at Fort Center by Thompson and Pluckhahn brings us closer to a fuller understanding of the Calusa and Lake People. In their paper, they introduce the concept of "persistent monumental places." They define such as "places where people continually return to alter, expand and reinvent the built environment." I view this assessment as the acknowledgment that to understand such places is to see the central role of beliefs organizing and reorganizing the ritual landscape. Thompson and Pluckhahn further state:

> The symbolic power and history of ritual at such sites effectively became resources that were tapped by individuals and groups who engaged in the remaking and the continued engagement in these places.

As I have already stated, nothing is more "persistent" than beliefs. Symbols live in the subconscious. Like beliefs, symbols operate outside of reason, which is why they are so powerful—powerful enough to have a great number of volunteers engaged in building and rebuilding for twenty-five centuries. I would add to this concept of persistent monumental places the supercharged symbolic/historical engagement by the people in a sacred place. I would also put forth that Thompson and Pluckhahn statement about such being resources that were tapped by individuals to be inaccurate. What marks the difference between the Calusa or Mayaimi and western societies was there was no concept of the individual. The Great Circle at Fort Center, for example, was probably the result of a vision by an individual, but all visions were the property of the group.

I was surprised that Thompson and Pluckhahn never mentioned the all-time winner of the persistent monumental Neolithic place in the New World. The record has been set by the Casma/Sechin cultures in northwestern Peru. Their engagement lasted a full 3,400 years. This remarkable achievement by fishing-hunter-gatherers is even more remarkable given that the region was a desert and one of the driest climates in the world. I am totally confident that once the right anthropologist works with the archaeological data, they will understand that the valley was a persistent sacred place.

When I finished my graduate work in teaching, not only did I not rely on a textbook, I chose to teach history from the present back in time. In terms of the Advanced Placement Histories, this allowed me to organize major, reoccurring themes and trace them back in time. For European History, there had been several paradigm shifts going back to the early Middle Ages. The most recent paradigm shift constructed by physicist Fritjof Capra in 1982 is where I started. Capra, the author of *The Tao of Physics*, published what I believe to be the most important work since the eighteenth century, *The Turning Point: Science, Society and the Rising Culture*. The new paradigm (worldview) put forth by Capra was the "systems view," a scientific view that incorporated "living systems." This view brought western civilization full circle back to a view held by all precivilized people, but rather with unreasonable beliefs organizing the viewpoint, it was now science.

The systems view in physics occurred due to the nature of life when viewing that atoms and subatomic particles did not conform to the mechanical view that has been the physical sciences as adopted by the works of Newton and Descartes. Atoms simply don't do or interact as the previous scientific view would predict. The resulting new view in Capra's words is that

> the new vision of reality we have been talking about is based on awareness of the essential interdependence of all phenomena—physical, biological, psychological, social and cultural.

Contrasted with the eighteenth-century view of the world,

> The systems view looks at the world in terms of relationship and integration. Systems are integrated wholes whose properties cannot be reduced to those of smaller units. Instead of concentrating on basic building blocks or basic substances, the systems approach emphasizes basic principles of organization.

Figure 5.2. Physicist Capra's "living systems" view mirrors that of the aboriginal societies of South Florida. The spider web is a symbol of the larger system in which each species or organism is interdependent and accounts for the integrity of the entire system. Photograph by sk howard, istockphoto.com.

Before I discuss the dramatic shift in the systems view of the role of the environment, it is important to note that in the systems view of systems within systems, all systems are self-organizing. Capra states that the interrelated systems that comprise the human system include and not exclude the psychological, social, and cultural. According to anthropologist Robin Fox, kinship systems like the ones used by the various groups in South Florida were natural systems and played a vital role in organizing the behaviors of individuals and groups, then and now. Going back to Dilts's view that the organizing agent for human social and cultural systems are the beliefs, the wholeness of systems is not only a major paradigm shift but also brings us back full circle to the view of the world held by the Calusa and their neighbors. Capra says in referring to the wilderness, "What is preserved in the wilderness is not the individual trees or organisms, but the complex web of relationships between them." The key word is *relationships*, which includes the root word *relations*.

Earlier in chapter 2, I discussed the work by the zoo archaeologists in Florida archaeology. One of the "three pillars" that guides zooarchaeology questions that they ask is flexibility. Citing the work of physicist Paul Weiss, Capra states that:

> Another important aspect of systems is their intrinsically dynamic nature. Their forms are not rigid structures but are flexible yet stable manifestations of underlying processes.

Referring back to my criticism of Sears, Widmer, and Marquardt given the longevity of Calusa and Mayaimi sociopolitical organization, it then would be reasonable to say it wasn't black or white. At the self-organizing level, they had to employ more fluid, dynamic, and flexible facets that incorporated egalitarian with hierarchal structures. Applying the systems view to the Calusa self-organizing system and not the environment determined their sociopolitical system. In dynamic living systems, the systems are not isolated from their environment. There is constant interaction. The interaction, though, as previously believed does not determine their organization.

Finally, my theory of a cultural synthesis and an amazing joint and cooperative relationship of the Calusa and Lake People is totally supported by the scientists who have adopted the systems view. Capra wrote:

> Detailed study of ecosystems over the past decades has shown quite clearly that most relationships between living organisms are essentially cooperative ones, characterized by coexistence and interdependence, and symbiotic in various degrees.

The problem of the Cartesian view that continues to dominate anthropology and archaeology is the view of human systems as somehow not being natural systems. The reason the work of anthropologist Robin Fox has been guiding all of my anthropological research is that he was really the first to view humans in species contexts. When you realize that humans are the cultural animal, that we use culture to self-organize, then it proceeds that culture is a natural system. The view of all the South Florida researchers were locked into models that viewed the Calusa or "Glade" cultures as static rather than dynamic. There is presently one, one single anthropologist in South Florida who consciously or not is viewing the subject of the "Glade"/Lake People utilizing the system view. In an important paper on the monumental ceremonial complexes built and rebuilt around Lake Okeechobee, Lawres used the work of Brian Yazzie Burkhardt to identify an important theme present in all those sacred landscapes—relatedness.

> The first of these themes is the "principle of relatedness" (Burkhardt 2004:16). In the context of Native American thought, this principle refers

> to an understanding that everything in a world is related and interconnected with everything in that world.

The application of the principle of relatedness moves the study of the Calusa and Mayaimi out of the dark ages of anthropology. I doubt, however, that Lawres will fully adopt the systems view in that Burkhardt believes the relatedness lives in the world of thought. Clearly the new physicists are stating emphatically that the relatedness is the reality and not a projection. To state this another way, if the Calusa and Lake People thought differently, the reality of their world would still be relatedness. The Capra book *The Turning Point* points out the science that proceeded from the Cartesian view has viewed all life as mechanistic parts. In 1997, Illinois archaeologist Thomas Edison, when referencing the results of the Language = Archeological culture philosophy, stated:

> The past has been dehumanized, mechanistic societies have been created that operate with functionality motivated, clockwork precision and that respond necessarily; only to external environmental stimuli.

Such assessments by a renown archaeologist of the failures of the current models employing a failure of vision can be viewed as the shift in paradigm affecting anthropology and archaeology. Referencing the literature, I have been able to view historically when the mechanistic view replaced the more human view. In Florida, it was immediately after World War II. Prior, while maybe romanticized somewhat, archaeologists still pondered the underlying beliefs of a culture as shown in the artifacts found.

Concluding, I cannot help but think about the living system now known as the Everglades and how the Calusa and their neighbors interrelated to the living system as contrasted with the culture today. Once the human systems changed from the original people to the migrants with their scientific view, things got worse and not better. The system is currently stressed to the max. Decades of applied science have taken a unique living system and put it on the UN "In Danger" List. If the new managers had viewed all life in the Everglades as relations, such damage would be immoral and unthinkable. To quote Wendell Berry once more, "A man with a machine and an inadequate culture, shakes more than he can hold."

In chapter 3, I discussed the predominant philosophy that has provided the theories used to explain the social organization, the group politics of the Calusa and Mayaimi. In the West, Darwin and Marx have had a major impact on social theories. Sociology had replaced cultural and physical anthropology. All humans were defined by society. Sociologists believed they solved the nature/nurture question. The Mayaimi and Calusa, I contend, give us a window into innovations by humans, social organizational strategies that were the result of tens of thousands of years subsisting in smaller hunter-gathering groups. As stated, I welcome Martin Byers's work and believe that some version of his dual organization model was at play in the Woodland period around 200 BC. I also believe, as Byers theorized, that this was the reemergence of this older adaptive strategy created to mitigate the problems developing by groups living in larger settled societies. The progressives rigidly believe that the only thing that mattered was the evolution of humans to large complex societies. Despite the repeated problems of social inequalities, crime, and violence, there is nothing in our past worth saving or worthy of a second look.

• 6 •

Viewing Prehistoric South Florida in a Global Context

Then God said, "Let us make man in our own image, after our likeness; and let them have dominion over the fish of the sea and over the birds of the air, and over the cattle, and over all the earth."

—Genesis 1:26

A sacred landscape formed the platform upon which early kings formed their authority. The juxtaposition of an area of high ground with a water source characterized this landscape. . . . It represented the place of creation, the source of life or the navel of the world, the moral locus of royal power.

—*The Olmec*, www.WorldHistory.biz

The act of creation was also important in and of itself, as indicated by the burying and rebuilding of several great circles at the same locale on the landscape.

—Victor Thompson and Thomas Pluckhahn, "Monumentalization of the Ritual Landscapes at Fort Center in the Lake Okeechobee Basin in South Florida"

Nonagrarian hunter-gathering societies are the oldest socioeconomic human societies in the world. Despite pressure, they have persisted in their way of life in every part of the world. Even now in the twenty-first century they can be found in a few remote environmental niches, but their days are numbered; as I recounted in my preface, with my encounter with native people in the Soviet Union in 1990. The Soviet State had started the process of dismantling the nomadic tribal people of the north. Little did they or anyone know that the

Soviet State would end in only two years' time. So, these autonomous people, whose way of life was over 150 centuries old, were ended by a modern state that lasted only seventy years. Here in the United States, archaeologists whose country is a mere two-and-one-half centuries old have been scrutinizing and passing judgment on indigenous societies like the Calusa, who thrived for a quarter of a millennium. Not all cultural systems succeed. Prehistory and history clearly reveal that there have been winners and losers. Humans employing natural systems of culture either adapt and continue or fail and cease to adapt. That was the legacy of Darwin's studies: not all species adaptations were successful. The end game then is the same today. A successful culture is one that persists for a long time.

Tool making we share with other hominids. Humans are the "cultural animal." It was culture that distinguished us from other creatures and made us godlike. It was culture that had the neocortex expand and develop overnight when applying Darwin's model. Human history is the story of how people adapted to different areas of the planet. Some cultural adaptations were successful; some were not so successful. Some regions had many resources, while other regions had sparse and few resources. When in regions of plenty, cities and civilizations developed and populations increased, and so did differences and conflict. Humans, being creatures of nature, develop, hopefully, the self-organizing social systems that match the ecology of the places they inhabit. While subsisting is the end game, humans use symbols, myth, imagination, and beliefs in the process. This book is an investigation into two distinctive groups of people, one presumed to be original, the other presumed to have been migrants who lived in a region with abundant resources cooperatively for twenty-five centuries. This record remains impressive when compared to not only neighboring cultures but also more so when compared to western civilization.

Starting out in the 1970s, I worked at a very young age for the Archaeology Department at the New Jersey State Museum. My principal job was to take the findings and prepare them for exhibitions. Every month, pottery parts came to me to figure out from the pieces the height and width and original form of the vessel. They were all pieces of a puzzle and entirely Eastern Woodland Tribal artifacts of the indigenous Lenni Lenape. Once in a while it was a trade good from a neighboring cultural region. In the summers I worked on the state-funded archaeological digs. I know how unromantic digging for artifacts really is. There is the heat, and the swampy areas with snakes and mosquitos. In short, I know why most archaeologists drink to excess.

My background and my major in college was fine arts. I consider myself fortunate to have made a living in visual arts my entire working life. My life and interests took a major turn when I turned forty and went blind in my left eye in 1989. The process of healing resulted in a shifting from making money and acquiring wealth and status to travel and spiritual awareness. Literally overnight, one experience opened doors to others. My life was filled with awe, wonder, and connectedness. In terms of my present research, early in this new life my younger sister moved to Florida. On my first visit, she drove me to Safety Harbor. There in a small park overlooking Tampa Bay was a tall ceremonial mound interrupting the seemingly flat terrain. After climbing the mound, I visited the small museum, which housed a selection of artifacts. I knew enough from my early years at the museum that a good portion of the stone artifacts were fashioned minerals from very far away. I was as dumbstruck then as much as today some twenty-eight years later at the size of the extensive trade networks from Florida to the Great Lakes. Later that year, I traveled to Ohio to visit the Great Serpent Mound (figure 6.1A) as well as various Hopewell and Adena sites. There I found the beautiful, fashioned shell ornaments and tools from Florida and the surrounding regions. Serpent Mound, now dated at 321 BC, is guaranteed to generate awe, curiosity, and inspiration in the average human. However, my life was now on spiritual autopilot.

Figure 6.1. Hereford Mappa Mundi (1290). Alamy Stock Photo.

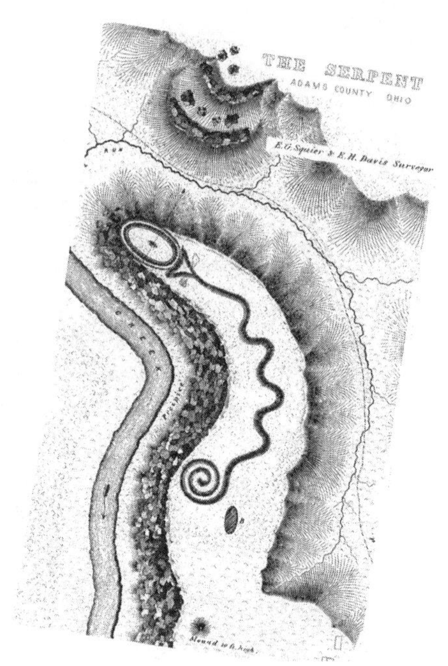

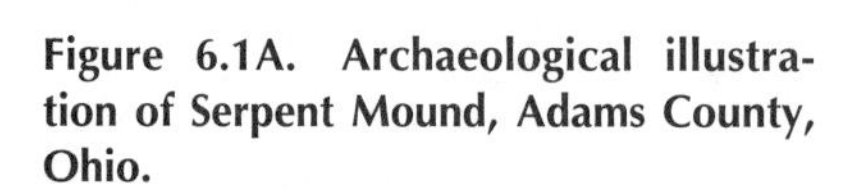
Figure 6.1A. Archaeological illustration of Serpent Mound, Adams County, Ohio.

In the early 1990s I became involved with the research of Dr. James Swan. Jim had a series of three global conferences organized around his research into "sacred places and spaces." His focus was global, and his conferences were attended by an incredibly diverse group of contributors and interested parties. It was at these conferences that I first met and interacted with shamans. The word *shaman* has a Siberian origin, but most people today would be surprised to know that shamans and their ancient prehistoric practices are alive and well in every corner of the modern world. Shamanism remains an incredible source of knowledge. My training, my subsequent beliefs and involvement with indigenous people, allows me to employ an emic study while researching early cultures. I remember one such celebrated Mayan shaman hosted by my friend Sandy Taylor, who shared what he knew with Mayan specialists at the University of Pennsylvania as well as nuclear physicists in Princeton in the mid-1990s. I went even further, training in core shamanic arts intensely for fifteen years with the Foundation for Shamanic Studies, and with the work of Michael Harner, Mill Valley, California. There are answers to big questions, such as: "Who built the serpent mound and why?" or for the present subject, "Why did the Lake People, the Calusa and the Tequesta, create great, dugout, circular ritual spaces as well as at least three monumental ceremonial complexes in South Florida?" Finally, "From where did the Calusa, the Tequesta, and Lake People originate, and why does it matter?" As I have put forth, the Calusa and Mayaimi "legacy" in the hands of modern anthropologists is diminishing, not increasing. What was, what is, has not changed, but only an overspecialized view lacking in knowledge, humanized models, and a true sense of awe and wonder. There has remained after 120 years the apparent need to view all the prehistoric people of South Florida in a global historical context. Sears, if he had researched other cultures for use in comparison, and Milanich and Widmer after him, would have been far more credible. And important.

There is presently a wealth of knowledge from over fifteen decades of anthropological and archaeological research of ancient cultures around the world. It becomes far easier to compare the culture or cultures being researched with other similar phenomena near or far. The anthropology of pre-Columbian Florida just might be a part of a larger cultural epoch, and not just southeastern North America. By comparison with other cultures, southern Florida may prove to bė uncommon or a unique cultural variation. While Thompson and Pluckhahn's work on Fort Center was significant, I was struck by the lack of other similar persistent places in support. Also, this duo, who have offered so much to affect the needed global context for Fort Center, also failed to illustrate that Fort Center may have been the geographical center of the South Florida indigenous world. In a chapter they wrote for *Early and Middle Woodland Landscapes of the Southeast* (2013), Thompson and Pluckhahn compared and contrasted three important ritual/village sites: Kolomoki, Crystal River, and Fort Center. They missed a very obvious similarity. All three were literally in the center of each culture's region. The pressing question then is: How were the religious leaders at the time, without geographical skills, able to divine the location? Why did the people build nine great circular ritual spaces in the center of the South Florida region?

Clearly the monumentalizing, the building of sacred landscapes in southern Florida, was a part of a global Neolithic epoch that originated with bands of hunter-gatherers in the Fertile Crescent in the fourth millennium BC and simultaneously in the New World in the Casma Valley and ending with the Mississippi mound cultures all over North America in 1600 AD, a persistent human epoch lasting over fifty centuries. In the Americas, one such persistent monumental place was coming to an end just when the Fort Center complex was beginning. The Casma River Valley in Peru beginning in 3600 BC was home to many monumental ceremonial complexes that were occupied and reoccupied for thirty-four centuries. The cultural region is identical to the Lake Okeechobee area of ceremonial complexes except for rainfall. For thirty-four centuries, the people who built these centers were dependent on fishing from the Pacific. They grew plants associated with extraction via fishing, but not for food. Originally, they did not produce ceramics. In short, they were desert dwellers who fished and had limited regional trade. So why did these people build these multiple monumental and communal complexes inland? Applying Dilts and Capra, to discern the answer, look toward their beliefs. Currently there are no anthropologists or archaeologists even interested in the Casma or Chechin cultures.

Look at any place on the globe where people built monumental works over long periods of time and you will find the origins in beliefs and religious rituals and rites. Mecca, an oasis with a spring, and that region in the Arabian Peninsula, was a sacred place long before the one God of Islam. The Indus River Valley, the sacred mount in Jerusalem, remains a testimony to persistent monumental places. In contrast, return to Sumer in what is now Iraq and you will find a few ruins and a great deal of sand. Places like Sumer are testimonials to beliefs that exceeded the limits of the environment. Places like Jerusalem are the truest example of Thompson and Pluckhahn's theory of persistent monumental places. Jerusalem also is the greatest proof of my theory about sacred places. Most people do not realize, for instance, that the earliest maps of Europe place Palestine as the center of their world (figure 6.1). Thompson and Pluckhahn understand this important point, even though their recent research avoids comparison on a global level and their continued dancing around the word *sacred*. In their chapter included in *Early and Middle Woodland Landscapes of the Southeast*, titled "Constituting Similarity and Difference in the Deep South," they remarked:

> Our exercise is entirely hypothetical but not outside the realm of possibility. Despite the distances between these sites, there are similarities in their artifact assemblages from shell and stone plummets to Crystal River—like pottery to suggest the possibility of direct if only sporadic contact through occasional pilgrimages or trading expeditions.

There is only one definition for the word *pilgrimage*, and that is the traveling to a sacred place. Had they availed themselves of other sacred sites during the Neolithic period, trade is a favored human activity, and thus the traveling sporadically to sacred places always provided the welcomed opportunity for trade. Therefore, it was never either/or but always both worship and trade.

The work by Thompson and Pluckhahn lacks credibility for reasons I will discuss in chapter 8. The similarities have resulted from their area of interest being these three sites. This is shades of Cushing always seeing similarities between his two important expeditions, the Zuni and the Calusa. For reasons I will discuss later, Fort Center was a regional religious site, a sacred place, one of several built over time that natives made pilgrimages to for generations going back to the Archaic period. They were, like Poverty Point before them, dedicated sacred ritual spaces and never villages. The large middens were the result of many feasts and not village life. They are world monuments to the power of beliefs, not to economic or political power that characterized the majority of large Neolithic complexes in the Old and New Worlds. From a global context, they were very special indeed.

Thompson and Pluckhahn, who did not include global phenomena in their local research, published their ideas on planned pilgrimages by religious followers a decade before Martin Byers's 2018 *Real Mound Builders* conclusions. Byers also never saw the global connections. The social organization strategy, hunter-gatherer in origin, that Byers believed reemerged in the Eastern Woodland areas in 200 BC, can be found in the beginnings of the first civilization in Mesopotamia. Byers's complimentary autonomous group were religious cult members. Today, cults have a very negative connotation. What Byers describes is in anthropological terms a nonfamiliar kinship group, a social organization by religious affiliation. William Sears, even with his many faulty interpretations of Fort Center, got one right. Sears stated that a priestly sect and their cult lived at Fort Center and was charged with its yearly operations. The first cities in the Fertile Crescent were built at the prehistoric temple mounds, religious sites maintained by a priestly group. Believers, hunter-gathering cult members, made planned pilgrimages to these centers. Civil leaders, the forerunners of kings, got their authority from the priestly cult. What resulted was shared power and responsibility for the sites. If you have not learned this lesson from the history of the Middle Ages in Europe, you missed a major development: the history of western civilization in the freeing of civil authority from its dependence on religion as the foundation for their legitimate power and authority.

Using global examples allows for the inclusion of trends and themes such as sacred places for researching phenomena such as that found in South Florida. The theory that initially drove my research of the Calusa and Mayaimi also came from world history, the principle of cultural synthesis. Cultural synthesis is defined as the process by which two or more cultures merge over time to produce new elements that did not previously exist in either separate cultures. It is much different than cultural diffusion. An example in pre-Columbian North America was the Hopewell/Mississippi culture. What suddenly appeared were mound-building, politically stratified settlements. The origin of these cultures was most likely the products of cultural synthesis. The spread of the new elements over the vast regions was the process of cultural diffusion.

My interest in cultural synthesis began when I was an undergraduate. The subject of my research was the Gothic cathedral. The Gothic cathedral was a whole new form of architecture, of cultural expression that did not exists prior in the Latin, Mediterranean-based, early Christian cultures. Nor did it exist in the northern, Germanic tribal cultures. Unlike the Byzantine churches that were dominating in the Mediterranean area, when Christianity moved north the place of worship changed dramatically. When you enter any of the great Gothic cathedrals, you enter a great old-growth forest. The columns soar upward, creating the experience of a great tree canopy. Even the light from the

Figure 6.2. The interior of the Gothic Cathedral in Prague, an example of monumental architecture resulting from the *cultural synthesis* of the southern Christian and the northern pagan cultures.

stained-glass windows is diffused and changes with the direction of the sun, exactly like light filters into the forest (figure 6.2).

When you look closely, all Gothic cathedrals have symbols that are characteristically pagan. Green Man, deer, and other forest creatures adorn the cathedral along with Christian saints. The merging of the south with the north was also the merging of the matriarchal values of the south with the patriarchal values of the north. The glue would not hold as history played out. During the religious wars after the Protestant Reformation, bands marched through the churches in the north, smashing all of the images of the Virgin Mary. When viewing the Neolithic period, especially its human origins in the Old World, cultural synthesis is a major theme. We have the oldest archaeological finds and data. What attracted these early archaeologists were the monumental buildings, temples, and tombs. Monumentality was a major theme of the new cultural expression resulting from cultural synthesis. The introduction of new beliefs, of a new religion, was another major theme as the cause for monumentality and cultural synthesis. I mentioned the walled city of Jerusalem. Originally, the Israelite city was built on an old religious site. There was no merging, no cultural synthesis. One culture and its beliefs replaced the other. Now the sacred city of three major world religions, the same process has been repeated. However, miles away in the port city of Haifa, Israel, on the Holy Mount Carmel is the religious center of the Bahai faith. The prophets of the Bahai faith merged all the world religions into a message of one man, one god, one religion. The merging of eight other monotheistic religions into one caused an entirely new sacred architecture, a nine-sided temple or house of worship. Consistent with ritual landscapes, the tombs of the twin Bahai prophets are part of the monumentalized religious complex.

Islam and Islamic architecture were the product of the cultural synthesis. To quote world historian Michael Wood:

> Like the others, Islam drew on Jewish, Christian, and Zoroastrian elements, but with its radical and democratic message, and its use of the Arabic language, it transformed the ancient cultures of the Near East.

When you enter one of these elaborate mosques, not unlike a Gothic cathedral, you are reminded of an oasis, but rather than physical renewal, it is a place of spiritual sustenance and renewal (figure 6.3).

This dramatic epoch called the Neolithic was revolutionary. Certain cultures sought to replace the beliefs and way of life of hunter-gathering people. Beginning with Samaria, each of these cities started with a mound and the beliefs of subsistent societies. In Michael Wood's series *Legacy*, Wood recounts the expedition of archaeologist F. W. Green working in the Nile Valley, who uncovered the remains of a large, circular mound of clean, white sand about 150 feet across and 8 feet tall dating back to the prehistoric. He argued that this mound, which symbolized the creation of the earth, was the ritual center of the Horus kings, the founders of Egypt (figure 6.4).

Wood continued to demonstrate that most of the great civilizations, including the New World, had their origins with a simple mound. Villages gave rise to large urban centers, even in the Americas. The earlier mounds were in comparison to the monumental architecture that proceeded them, and were built to human scale. What is unique about the mound complexes built in South Florida is while the expanse was of monumental scale, the height was still human scale. At Fort Center, the Great Circle was monumental in its radius. However, as a place of worship, the depth of the circle was only six feet deep, the height of an adult male. The participants in the rituals in the Great

Figure 6.3. Interior of a mosque. Photograph by tunart.

Figure 6.4. Drawing of *Creation Mound* at Giza archaeological site, Nile Valley, Egypt. andrewcollins.com

Circle were below the surface, just enough not to be distracted by the world around them. The mortuary mound, charnel platform, and pond similarly were human scale. Sears concluded that the pantheon of carved wooden beasts and birds were on posts, and that they were six feet in height. Again, critical elements in that ritual place were in balance with the human scale (figure 6.5). One can conclude about the monumentalization of the landscape when compared to function. In architecture, form follows function. Hierarchically organized societies needing to symbolically convey and maintain power and authority built taller and larger structures. They also designed the space to control the focus. By this I am referring to platformed mounds or pyramids that physically exalt the divine leader. Each of those large structures had carefully designed courts below for the adoring masses. Certainly, Cushing discovered and made records of Calusa versions of this architecture for maintaining an exalted rank of Calusa chiefs, but the common space and plazas are remarkably different. The Calusa and lake area spaces were decisively more interactive. I have been interested in the scale of and interactiveness of ritual spaces in North America since my visit to Serpent Mound in Ohio. The expanse of the effigy mound is immense. When you move around the mound, especially the spiraled tail of the serpent, the height and width are perfect for human ritual interaction (figure 6.1A). The scale is human scale.

When comparing the great ritual earthworks of the Calusa and Mayaimi with others in the Americas and the Old World, they are unique. They are

Figure 6.5. Archaeological reconstruction of the Fort Center mortuary mound and pond complex before it was destroyed. Ted Ehmann, 2019.

very special because they are a totally new expression resulting from the merging of two different aboriginal cultures. You can witness this coming together by first analyzing the strictly Calusa-style mounds, circular ditches, causeways, canals, and ponds. The layouts were asymmetrical and give the appearance of being random, lacking in geometric order and balance. When looking at the Fort Center site, the largest structure is the Great Circle. The circle is totally symmetrical, ordered, centered, and distinctly feminine. East of the Great Circle and built after the circle was the mortuary complex. The design is distinctly Calusa with the inclusion of the charnel pond, but it has a balanced, symmetrical design that is borrowed from the Mayaimi style. Further east and south of Fort Center are two sites with eight and nine raised causeways leading to burial mounds. None of the mounds connect to each other, and causeways radiate from a plaza that has a massive platform mound. You will find no similar ritual complex design anywhere else on the planet. This entirely new design was Big Mound City (figure 6.6), which was started around 1000 AD. This date corresponds to Sears's work that showed the mortuary complex at Fort Center was not used after 800 AD. While Nathan Lawres probably wants to say the function of both new ritual complexes had to do with the study of the stars and the planets, I believe, short of their excavations, that both were the venerated burial mounds of the clans or native kinship groups in prehis-

Figure 6.6. Archaeological reconstruction of the Big Mound City archaeological site. Ted Ehmann, 2019.

toric South Florida. My theory is based on my research showing the people migrated from the Eastern Woodland areas of North America. Those tribes had eight or nine distinct clans. Because there are no ruins that emphasize powerful chiefdoms, clans and their distinguished ancestors would have been the organizing force.

Pluckhahn believes that circular ritual space at Fort Center functioned to mitigate tensions between individuals and kinship groups as populations grew in villages (figure 6.7). But I cannot disregard that Carr documented eight or nine great circles throughout the entire region. When you apply form follows function, each circle would hold 1,500 individuals. For comparison, the Great Circle at Fort Center was one-and-one-quarters bigger than the plaza in front of St. Peter's Square in Vatican City, Rome. No villages in the interior were that large. Therefore, the ritual spaces may have been gathering places for clans and kindship allied people from over the entire region for use in burials and other life-affirming events. Therefore, I am inclined to now believe that the great circles functioned to build interclan unity and maintain a strong kindship and identity. Who could marry, and to whom, was a primary kindship or clan function. So, marriages and feasting would require regional ritual spaces.

When Cushing unearthed Calusa artifacts at the Key Marco site, he found a repeated symbol carved in wood amulets and in larger altar tablets.

Figure 6.7. Archaeological reconstruction artist Dee Turman's concept of the Fort Center archaeological site. From *The Illustrated Encyclopedia of Native America Mounds & Earthworks*, Gregory J. Little (2008), with permission from Eagle Wing Books, Inc.

He recognized the symbol immediately from his expeditions in the Southwest. The symbol is a circle with a cross: the world and the four sacred directions. My research these past twenty-five years has found this symbol on all continents and a wide variety of regions: the Middle East, Europe, the Far East, Africa, and the Americas. This organizing symbol represented the world and the essential unity of and relatedness of all life (figure 6.8). It was and remains a sacred symbol that represents a profound and unifying belief. A new emerging belief transitioned in the Americas from the Archaic period through the Woodland periods, a belief that functioned to mitigate tensions and suppress violence.

Regarding the topic of violence and warfare in South Florida, anthropologists and archaeologists have historically been reluctant to record examples of ritualized violence and warfare or discuss the subject all together. This is interesting because there are primary sources during the European period that describe intergroup violence, including a graphic depiction in an early etching by Theodor de Bry (1620) (figure 6.9). A major theme in human history, violence and warfare has been a touchy subject for generations of liberal-mindset

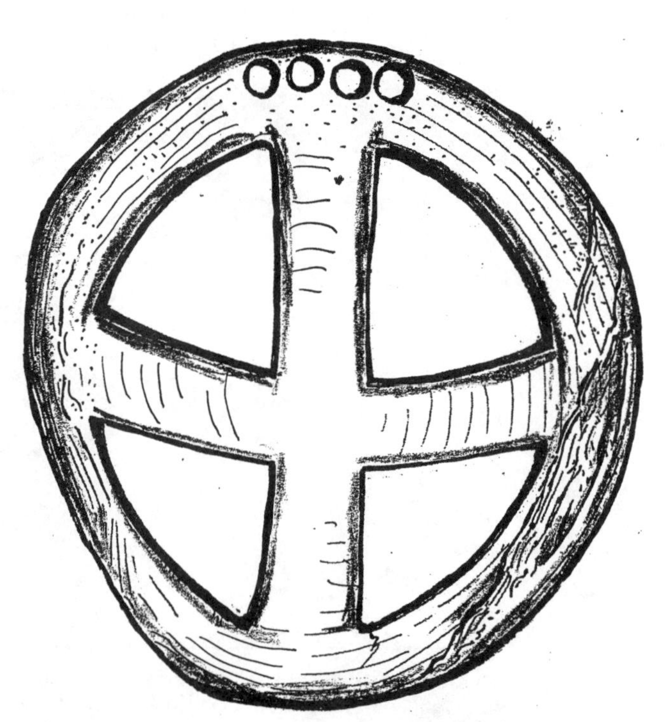

Figure 6.8. Drawing of Calusa shell gorget from Key Marco site. Drawing based on a sketch by Frank Hamilton Cushing (1896).

Figure 6.9. Engraving by Theodor de Bry, 1620. alamy.com.

researchers of Native Americans who would rather advance a false narrative of the noble savage than deal with the facts.

In 1968, anthropologist Napoleon Chagnon published his research on the Yanomami, a Brazilian/Venezuelan group of hunter-gatherers. He was immediately attacked by people in the field for his descriptions of intergroup violence, descriptions that were painstakingly factual. Recently, an article written for the *New York Times Magazine*, February 13, 2013, by Emily Eakin, recalled the controversy:

> In turning the Yanomami into the world's most famous "unacculturated" tribe, Chagnon also turned the romantic image of the "noble savage" on its head. Far from living in harmony with one another, the tribe engaged in frequent chest-pounding duels and deadly inter-village raids, violence or threat of violence dominated social life. The Yanomami, he declared, "live in a state of chronic warfare."

The following year, a global collection of do-gooders organized a non-profit organization to defend primarily the reputation of indigenous people. The group named "Survival" currently hosts a website that features a section titled "The Myth of the 'Brutal Savage,'" where they out anthropologists who describe violence in native societies.

As I discussed in chapter 1, bias and predisposition run rampant in anthropology and archaeology. Pennsylvania State University professor George R. Milner in a 2007 comprehensive and systematic review of violence and warfare in prehistoric North America remarked about eastern researchers:

> North America archaeologists for several decades prior to the 1990s steadfastly clung to a romantic view of a peaceful prehistory, an idea with deep roots in Western thought about humankind's natural state.

In Florida, a perfect example would be Jerald Milanich's *Archaeology of Precolumbian Florida* (1994). Considered to be the most comprehensive and detailed study of all the tribes and cultures, it consists of four hundred pages and not one mention of warfare or violence. Recently, the editor Alisse Waterston of *Open Anthropology*, a publication of the American Anthropological Association, wrote:

> Violence is neither timeless, nor inevitable. In its specificity, there is nothing inherently natural about violence.

True anthropologists know this to be false. There has always been human violence. There is every indication that there will always be violence into the future of our species. As Robin Fox has always stated, humans are the only species with a "violent imagination." Humans add meaning to violence and thus ritualize through symbolism individual or collective acts of violence. As a historian, I know perfectly well that the study of warfare is the study of ritualized violence. To the Alisse Waterstons of the world, all I can say is that humans are natural, they are a biological species, and because humans have always been violent, then violence is natural.

Not wanting to once again write a book about prehistoric people in South Florida sans all references to violence and warfare, I will now join my research to the global history by citing some examples. There will not be much due to the previously stated avoidance in the research. Further hindering a respectable presentation on the subject is the lack of burial analysis in Florida, which I discussed in chapter 2. While accidents did happen, there are skull and skeletal realities found in burial mounds that could only be interpreted as the result of combat, victims of a raid, or the severed head of a trophy from conquest. The earliest account can be found in the the late nineteenth-century archaeology of Clarence B. Moore and Frank Hamilton Cushing. Cushing remarks on remains he excavated from the Safford Burial Mound at Tarpon Springs in 1896, of two internments of:

> individuals who had met their death by violence as revealed by the broken condition of their skulls, the marks traceable upon their bones, or the presence of arrow points.

Clarence Moore described numerous human remains at both Thomas Mound in Hillsborough County and Cockroach Key Mound in Manatee County that had suffered violent attacks. Moore wrote of a female skeleton with shark teeth imbedded in her bones from a war ax weapon. What was common practice by early archaeologists abruptly stopped by 1960. Without more Calusa burial archaeology, we will be in the dark as to the amount of internal conflicts or warfare with other chiefdoms that occurred during their twenty-five centuries. Florida state archaeologists removed over one hundred individual burials from the Aqui Esta Mound in Punta Gorda, Florida, in the 1970s and never investigated the remains or made notes on the existence of violence, a total waste. More than likely warfare existed throughout North America as populations increased, wars increased, and defense determined survival. There again, clans and their warriors were vital for a collective defense against aggressive neighbors.

Cushing was fascinated with the symbols of warfare found in the artifacts from Key Marco. The majority of his unpublished paper, titled "Key Marco Types," is about war symbols and warrior protection symbols. Due to his experience with Southwestern indigenous archaeology, he brought to his analysis of war and warrior symbols in the Calusa culture a wealth of cross-cultural knowledge. Most astute were his comments on the hatchet and war club. Cushing concluded that the Calusa, like other native cultures, believed in peace through strength. What we would think were symbols of war were so designed to project enough strength that any likely rivals would think twice before attacking. His comments on "burying the hatchet" demonstrated the complex psychology behind and the nature of these ancient symbols. Carrying the idea further to modern times, you could say "burying the missile."

Another source was the work of Jeffrey McClain Mitchem at Safety Harbor, which I highlighted in chapter 2. Clearly his identification of remains found at the Tatham Mound speak both to the status attributed to precontact warriors and to the victims of postcontact violence. Mitchem found in an isolated burial mound 480 an elite, adult male individual whose artifacts were:

> decorated with Mississippian warfare/cosmogony iconographic motifs buried with trophy skulls.

Trophy skulls, those being the skulls of the defeated taken from the vanquished in armed conflicts, were universal by tribal cultures around the world. They were commonplace in Florida throughout prehistory but rarely referred to as such. Typically, the archaeologist would simply refer to "a single adult skull" that was found. True, not all skulls found in burial mounds were "trophy skulls." That is why the entire context of the burial is required. In another mound 133, Mitchem found:

> two bones from the post contact stratum. Both of these secondary deposits exhibited evidence of injury inflicted by an edged metal weapon, or sword.

There are signs that at least in South Florida, archaeologists are breaking with the past and conducting research on the topic of ritualized violence. In a chapter titled *Its Ceremonial, Right?* Ryan J. Wheeler and Robert S. Carr use the subject of animal sacrifice found at the Miami Circle in Dade County, Florida, to cover the gamut from animal sacrifice to human sacrifice and trophy skulls in South Florida prehistory. While they fail to make the connection that in terms of the beliefs of the people in South Florida, animals were relatives of humans and thus the sacrifice of an animal was essentially the same as that of a fellow human, their research on the topic is significant. Milner's systematic research of pre-Columbian violence in eastern North America from the Archaic period up to the European encounters revealed times of increased occurrences, as well as lulls in violence. It is now possible to reference this research and apply these models to regional studies. Milner's research, using archaeological evidence data from the Middle Archaic from 6000 BC to 3000 BC, showed a high occurrence of violence among sedentary hunter-gatherer societies. By the end of the Archaic, a period defined by population stagnation, differences between hunter-gathering groups intensified. This trend continued until the Middle Woodland period from 100 BC to 400 AD, when it totally reversed itself. This period, besides showing major changes due to agriculture, was also marked by intensive trade. This period is when Martin Byers believes that the religious kinship organizations reemerged. Going back to the Neolithic period, sacrifices were common. We need to look no further than the Old Testament. I would venture that sacrifices associated with the Calusa had their connection to the religious cults that reemerged. I believe that this cult emerged earliest in South Florida, evidence being the building of the Great Circle in 800 BC.

According to Byers, these cults were assigned the responsibility for maintaining the "purity" of the territories. Something like the first ecologists, the increased populations and groups living in permanent villages had an increasing effect on the environment. "Civilization" treated the environment and the natural resources (believed to be relations) much differently than nomadic hunter-gatherers. Many religious rites, including sacrifice, would have been used to purify the circle of all living things. When the Europeans came with their foreign practices and religion, the need to ensure the purity of the territories must have been at an all-time high. The lull in violence did not last very long, however; by the Late Woodland period from 400 AD to 1000, culture became more technologically self-reliant. Chiefdoms had also become more powerful, controlling more land, people, and resources. Conflicts and rivalries between chiefdoms and political elites seeking more power and influence often defined intragroup tensions.

Pertaining to inter- or intragroup ritual violence and warfare in Florida, what we really know is from the historical record. If you think that for, instance, the Timucua, the northeast neighbors of the Calusa and Mayaimis, were a basically peaceful, self-determined collective of fisherman and pottery makers, think again. There is an account from a French explorer René Goulaine de Laudonnière, who witnessed in 1564 that after a battle, Timucua warriors cut the limbs off the defeated, broke the bones, and put the bones on a fire to dry. They then hung the bones with the scalp, placing them on the ends of their spears to carry them home in triumph.

So far, I have shown that the Calusa and the Lake People were very religious. But any true ethnological account must deal with the other nature of man. This is especially important when viewing both groups in a global Neolithic context. European accounts have shown the Calusa to be fierce people. There are no similar accounts of the people who thrived around Lake Okeechobee during the same period. One thing confirmed by the archaeology of the area is that very few arrowheads, spears, and knives have been found to date, a particular fact in archaeology being noteworthy and confirmed by the accounts of Escalante Fontaneda in his memoirs. He remarked that the Lake People lacked minerals. He was referring to minerals used for tools and weapons. Therefore, these people who lived in villages of thirty people, spread over a large area, were in need of defense. This supplies yet another important function of a Calusa and Mayaimi alliance.

A need for defense is underscored by facts from Sears's excavations at the mortuary complex at Fort Center. Sears's excavation unearthed evidence of a violent time in the history of the Lake People and the Fort Center ceremonial complex. While Sears attributed all the facts to accidents, there was sufficient evidence that what happened was a deliberate raid on the site with the expressed purpose to loot and desecrate an important religious center. Because of Sears's dating, the raid occurred between 700 AD and 900, a particularly violent time in Europe when Viking armies raided, looted, and desecrated holy centers in England. Pennsylvania State University professor George R. Milner surveyed records of warfare in southeastern North America and confirmed that the period when the Calusa and Mayaimi built the Great Circle and the mortuary complex was a characteristically peaceful time. He also found that the time of the raid on Fort Center was the start of a new renewal in Native American violence.

The facts as published by Sears were that there was a fire on part of the elaborately carved charnel platform. The platform was compromised by the fire and, as a result, the platform, effigies, and three hundred bundled human remains fell into the pond. Around the same time residents at the complex did spring cleaning and threw rubbish and "a lot of feces" down into the pond as well. At some point, the latter half of the burials were taken out of the pond and buried in the burial mound. From then on, the mortuary complex was abandoned, and except for a living residence, it was never used. I believe a related fact just discovered by Nathan Lawres and Matthew Colvin (2017) while dating Big Mound City: the construction began on that ceremonial complex within one hundred years of the discontinuance of the Fort Center complex.

David H. Dye and Adam King wrote a research paper in 2007 titled "Desecrating the Sacred Ancestor Temples: Chiefly Conflict and Violence in the American Southeast." They supply a wealth of documented raids on mortuary complexes by Native Americans. Their examples, which included evidence of desecration of burial complexes, match the same history found around the world. Critical to chiefly conflicts were orchestrated raids intended to delegitimize their competitors and win over supports. Most likely the rise in power of the Calusa in the south and their alliance with the Mayaimi was noticed and feared. My theory regarding this period at Fort Center is further supported by the incredible number of remains on the charnel platform, a clear indication of a sudden increase in mortality probably owing to violent raids on the Lake People's villages. In the next chapter, I will discuss the other chiefdoms in Florida at that time.

• 7 •

Sacred Places and Sacred Spaces

> To encounter the sacred is to be alive at the deepest center of human existence. Sacred places are the truest definitions of the earth. They stand for the earth immediately and forever; they are its flags and shields.
>
> —N. Scott Momaday

Part of my transformation initiated by the blindness in 1989 was a desire to return to school. I enrolled at the College of New Jersey to complete my bachelor's in art but with an intensive adding of the social sciences. One of the many doors that opened for me was anthropology. This new area was jump-started by a used dollar paperback titled *Adventures in Anthropology* by Robin Fox. Soon it became my dream at age forty-one to earn my degree in art and do graduate work with Dr. Fox at nearby Rutgers University. Well, that never happened. Ironically, his ex-wife was my anthropology professor at TCNJ, and despite my constant sourcing of Robin Fox, her ex, I did well. During those two years I read everything anthropological, and because of my artistic right-brain dominance I saw relationships and patterns others in the field failed to notice. One such author was Victor Turner, whose writings on rites and the ritual gave me many of the insights necessary for the research on the Calusa and Lake People. In keeping with my cross-cultural, interdisciplinary, and global viewpoint, I will now share with you where the Calusa and their culture fit within world history, but as promised, while mirroring a trend that was global at the time, they were more distinguished than others.

Everyone who studies world history knows that there are some brief pages on the Paleolithic period (Stone Age). When I taught world history, I wrote an entire unit with hundreds of pages. Robin Fox being my favorite and most trusted anthropologist believes that all we really need to understand about humans can be found in the "Paleo Terrific." With the end of the nineteenth century came the birth of sociology. Sociologist were uncomfortable with continuing socially disruptive behaviors in modern societies. Before many of the major questions about humans could be answered, this offspring of the noble pursuit of the study of man killed the father and insisted that all questions should be focused on complex societies. Therefore, unless you had me as your instructor, you got two pages of 99 percent of human experience on the planet. Suddenly and without transition, you begin the story with nomadic tribes living subsistent in the "Fertile Crescent" where the Tigris and Euphrates rivers join in present-day Iraq. But again, those who own the history and control the narrative are so quick to get us to the ancient Greeks, believing that they play a role in "western civilization." The Mesopotamian civilization ended up with writing, laws, agriculture, and cities. For someone who now wishes to view the Calusa and Glades people in a global context, it is necessary to slow things down and view not only how this cultural revolution came to be but also how its origin was one of many not shared but independently established around the globe, a global phenomenon.

If you do your research on Mesopotamia, there was a sacred site known by the nomadic peoples of the region for hundreds of centuries. A cult of priests maintained the site: they organized the construction of ceremonial spaces, preserved and performed the sacred rites and seasonal rituals, and conducted the burial rituals all while worshipping the gods and assuring them favor. The spiritual center was shared also in the communal center secular. The seasonal coming together of diverse peoples allowed for the sharing of ideas and technology, the forming of alliances, and the mediums of exchange and trade. Eventually this is what we refer to in Anthro 101 as the "strong man," and seeing opportunity the strong man created a symbiotic relationship with the cult of the priest, offering the priest safety and wealth in exchange for their anointing as temporal leader. This first of many occurred sometime around 5500 BC. The Sumerians are instructive to later chapters in that widescale domestication of plants and animals, and the agriculture and urban development there where regional sacred sites—mounds, mounts, springs, and lakes—were recognized by such bands, then tribes of hunter-gatherers. In truth our ancestors viewed the entire landscape as sacred and its inhabitants in all kingdoms—animal, plant, mineral, and clouds—as spirit. Over time, however, depending on where you roamed or lived on the planet, there were places designated as sacred places. A mount in Judea that would become Jerusalem was such a place to nonmonotheistic people before King David. You could argue that while there was great diversity in stories, gods, ancestors, and memory of the early people who gathered at these sacred sites, the sacred site was held in common and as such provided the fertile ground for building not only a civilization but

Figure 7.1. Snaefellsness National Park, Iceland. istockphoto.com.

Figure 7.2. Labyrinth carved in lava rock. Snaelfellsness National Park. From Ted Ehmann.

also, in some cases, an empire. It was at the sacred mountain, Mount Sinai, that God gave the Ten Commandments to Moses (figure 7.3).

Pluckhahn in a 2004 paper focused on larger villages in the Deep South region of North America around 100 to 500 AD applies the traditional anthropological concept of sacred versus secular designations to constructed elements common to all villages at the time. He emphasizes that sacred and ritual sites functioned to mitigate inherent tensions—individual and group—as these villages grew in population and size. His study, besides using secular versus sacred ceramics, discussed partitioned places within the village. Sacred structures studied were plazas and burial mounds. He did not include any villages in South Florida in his study, even though he is a South Florida anthropologist and later would coauthor a study of Fort Center.

I am introducing a new term and concept. You will not find references to "sacred places" anywhere in the literature. From its origin as a social science, cultural anthropology has included many comparisons, such as Pluckhahn's on culturally designated sacred things as opposed to secular things. But even on his work at Fort Center, the term *sacred* is never used. Cultural anthropologists refer to sacred places as constructed ritual landscapes, burial mounds,

Figure 7.3. Lithograph of Moses and his followers below the sacred mountain, Mount Sinai. istockphoto.com.

temple mounds, and such. None have ventured to research natural features: lakes, springs, rivers, mountains, and valleys as sacred. Historians have had no problem discussing how people in ancient times built centers or made repeated pilgrimages to places they knew were sacred. I have no problem sharing that I among many people from diverse cultures know places to be sacred. It was Pluckhahn, along with Victor Thompson, who first argued for the prehistoric historical significance of South Florida being host to four monumental complexes for religious ritual (figure 7.4). Besides the immense size of all four complexes and their large earthworks, they had their location and proximity to the Great Lake, originally called by the name of the people who lived there, Lake Mayaimi (figure 7.4B).

In 2005, after twenty-five years of trying, I arrived at the extreme western tip of the Snaefellsnes Peninsula of Iceland. This remote landscape had been calling out to me for some time. If you have never had a place call to you, it is difficult to empathize. Where I grew up and lived, New Jersey, places that called to you were Atlantic City and Disney World. Readers know Snaefellsnes as the volcano in Jules Verne's novel where they enter to journey to the center of the earth (figure 7.1). Hiking between the waters of the Atlantic and the base of the extinct glacier-capped volcano, I discovered a large, man-made ritual space, a labyrinth cut out of volcanic rock (figure 7.2). Upon further research, I learned that the earlier inhabitants frequently used the area for numerous yearly rites and rituals. The area remains the most sacred place I have ever encountered. By that I mean the veil that separates the spiritual world or dimension with the physical is extremely thin to nonexistent. Snaefellsnes National Park is a place where the gods and spirits are in your face, up close and personal. Returning to the subject, the maze is an example of people building sacred spaces/ritual spaces next to or adjoining a sacred place, not unlike Fort Center, beginning with the great circle sacred space near the Great Lake sacred place. Even today, when I first made my exhausting hike to the Fort Center site on Fisheating Creek, I felt the sacred. Within minutes, I was renewed. Sacred places have the power to renew and to heal. I sprained my foot badly while sketching waterfalls in the southern Appalachian Mountains. My foot got so bad that I feared I would have to cancel the balance of my trip. The next day, while limping to another waterfall in the ancestral lands of the Cherokee people, I discovered a single fall descending from a limestone cliff. I put my foot under the small, cold shower. The foot was 100 percent better in fifteen minutes.

The Ten Commandments, the moral code that is the basis of western civilization, were given to humans on Mount Sinai. It matters little to the discussion whether you believe the story or not. Humans since prehistory believe in sacred places. Even the new Systems View physicists understand

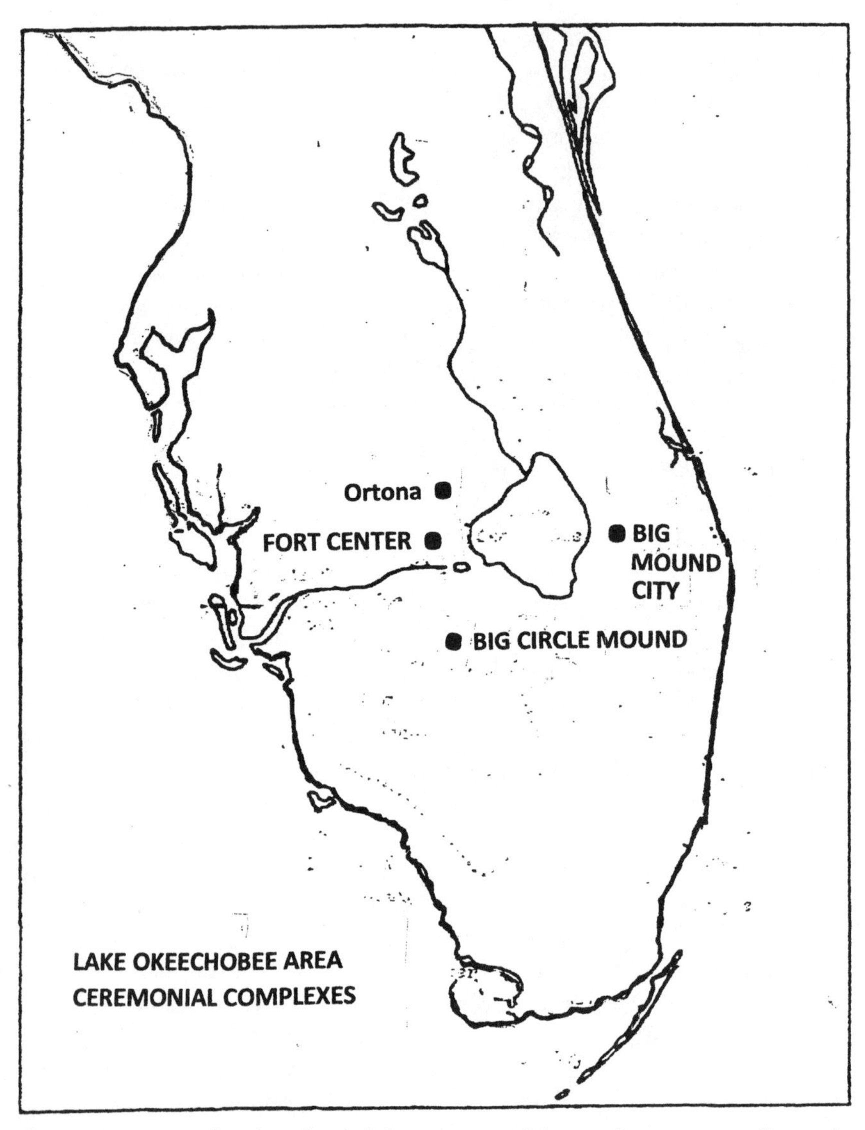

Figure 7.4. Map showing the religious ceremonial complexes surrounding Lake Okeechobee, South Florida region. Ted Ehmann, 2019.

Figure 7.4B. Photograph of Lake Mayaimi, now called by the Cherokee word *Okeechobee*. The Florida Department of State.

that the psychological is a real component of a natural system. In and around present-day Citrus and Marion counties, these headwaters leading to the Gulf of Mexico are dotted with Bay, Rainbow, Homosassa, Silver, and Crystal Springs. The archaeology of these springs illustrates their long and continued occupation. Sears's excavations at Fort Center unearthed large amounts of Crystal River ceramics, linking them to highly prized grave goods. Except for Safety Harbor, no monumental ritual constructions were built by the early people near these springs. The mineral spring at Safety Harbor named "Spring of the Holy Spirit" is the site of a large ceremonial mound built by the Tocobaga people. Springs were the sacred places of the pagan/tribal cultures of Europe that were adopted by the Romans and later by the Christians. That the Spanish called the springs at Safety Harbor a religious name attests to the persistent consideration of this natural occurrence as a key component of a ritual landscape.

Florida is significant for its large number of intrinsically historic sacred places. While it lacks mountains and valleys, Florida makes up in the water department. Besides the Great Lake, Florida has the largest concentration of springs in the world. There are more than two hundred springs in the district north and northwest of Tampa Bay. Two important Paleo-Indian to words were joined Woodland period sites, Warm Mineral Springs and Little Salt Springs (figure 7.5) in South Florida, are more than springs; they are gigantic

Figure 7.5. Aerial photograph of Little Salt Springs, Sarasota County, Florida.

sinkholes. Evidence since the mid-twentieth century reveals the sites were often used for ritual purposes, including underwater burials.

Across the Atlantic during their Middle Ages, the most sacred place was the Holy Lands. Regionally, the established sacred places were those like springs, rivers, and valleys known as sacred from the tribal people. In order to establish Christian holy places, they were built on or adjoining older sacred places, a common theme in world history. Another common theme was the investing of political leaders with spiritual authority. In the Old World and then in the Americas, there appeared some form of the "divine right of kings." The spiritual leaders anoint and legitimize the supreme power of the king and the ruling family and class. This process essentially created a symbiotic relationship between the spiritual class and the warrior class. Typically, before long the king seized more of the power from the religious leaders, causing them to be subordinate. But as in all things cultural, there were many cultural variations on this theme.

Calusa researcher William Marquardt weighed in on this theme and how he believed it played out in South Florida.

> The spiritual and the material realms made up a seamless world for the south Florida native people. According to documents, common people believed in the absolute power of the Calusa leader. His power was a function of—and proof of—his identification with both the practical and spiritual of their everyday world. As their leader prospered, the land and the waters would bring forth their abundance.

Marquardt states further:

> To separate the Calusa leader from the spiritual world was to destroy him as an authority figure and deny him his reason for existence.

This view is suspect based on several very significant facts about the Calusa and their region. First, while there were permanent settlements, the Calusa and their neighbors were fishing-hunter-gatherers. They remained fishing-hunter-gatherers for twenty-five centuries. As Poverty Point anthropologist Jon Gibson logically surmised, it is hard to believe a historically egalitarian people would need or agree to an all-powerful (temporal and religious) leader. Second, the religious centers were deliberately removed and built away from the center of temporal authority. The political center of Calusa authority was on Mound Key in Estero Bay, while the religious centers were inland around Lake Okeechobee. Finally, there are no examples of king as divinity temple mounds at the ritual centers. These you find elsewhere in abundance in Central and South America. As Pluckhahn adequately illustrates, the entire Deep South region built circular egalitarian ritual plazas and not mounds to establish divine kings.

There is more evidence, based on Victor Turner's work, that the Calusa and Lake People survived and flourished for twenty-five centuries not because of the inequality present in a top-down hierarchical political-religious system of organization but because of the wise employment by the Calusa leaders of rites and a "ritual process" that yearly blurred those distinctions. The great circle built, destroyed, and rebuilt by the people at Fort Center was the sacred space, the ritual landscape where all entered and found communion, comitas, and community. Further study of the South Florida region will most likely give us a picture of Calusa leadership, power, and authority that is quite different from Marquardt's assertion. Once you accept that the Calusa and Mayaimi joined forces and together they built the monumental ritual complexes of Fort Center, Big Mound City, and Big Circle Mound, the Calusa leader could not have been identified with the spiritual realm. Practically speaking, they did not have to in order to establish or maintain authority. Usually those cultural leaders who employed this device typically ruled many factions and had more limited resources than the Calusa. Such ruling families also organized around spiritual hunter-gathering globally to build permanent settlements, beliefs, and practices.

The hallmark of this epoch and its fishing-hunter-gathering was that the people learned through many generations' cooperation. The cooperative and reciprocal ethics instilled allowed for volunteers to engage in the construction of ritual places. As stated earlier, the entire Neolithic and what we study as world history or western civilization begins with sacred places and spaces.

• 8 •

Viewing the Calusa and Mayaimi in a Local Context

Ancestors of these native Floridians had been here for 12,000 years. Over the millennia many different cultures had developed, adjusting to different environments and dealing with the problems and challenges presented by increasing populations, new ideas and innovations.

—Jerald T. Milanich, *Florida's Indians from Ancient Times to the Present*

It is my feeling that careful linguistic analysis of the above forms, as well as several other toponyms for which no translation is provided by Escalante Fontaneda, indicates that six ethic/political units did, indeed speak dialects of a single language, which I refer to as Calusa.

—Julian Granberry, *The Calusa: Linguistic and Cultural Origins and Relationships*

Prior to 2011, anthropologists conducting their work in Florida had to limit their assessments to conclusions based solely on ceramic artifacts. That is because a subdivision of anthropology, linguistics, had not weighed in with their analysis—for 115 long years. Who lived in prehistoric Florida, where and how long they lived there and how big their cultural areas where, was determined primarily on dated ceramic artifacts. But as John Hann once wisely stated, a culture is far more than a collection of pot sherds. Now that Granberry has completed his initial linguistics data, prehistoric Florida into the seventeenth century looks very different. What linguistics can contribute is a knowledge of the origins of native people. While when dealing with a myriad of possibilities because of the thousands of years involved, linguistics can geographically pinpoint with accuracy the mother tongues for many languages and dialects. Over the past 120 years, many anthropologists, which include Sears, believed that the majority of tribes in South Florida came here via the Antilles from south-central America. Language doesn't lie, and now we know that the Calusa and its neighbors, including the Tocobaga (Safety Harbor) in South and Central Florida, spoke a dialect of Tunica, a language spoken by the people who built Poverty Point in northeastern Louisiana (figure 8.1). Granberry is fairly sure that the Calusa were a final wave of migrants of a great diaspora from that region during the Late Archaic period. The Calusa's neighbors and allies in South Florida were the Mayaimi, Tequesta, and the Ais. All of Granberry's theories are supported by the memoirs of Hernando de Escalante Fontaneda, a Spaniard shipwrecked and forced to live with the Calusa in the sixteenth century. Clearly by the sixteenth century, the Calusa were the dominant culture in the region south of Charlotte Harbor, but it is unlikely that they eradicated the native tongues of their neighbors.

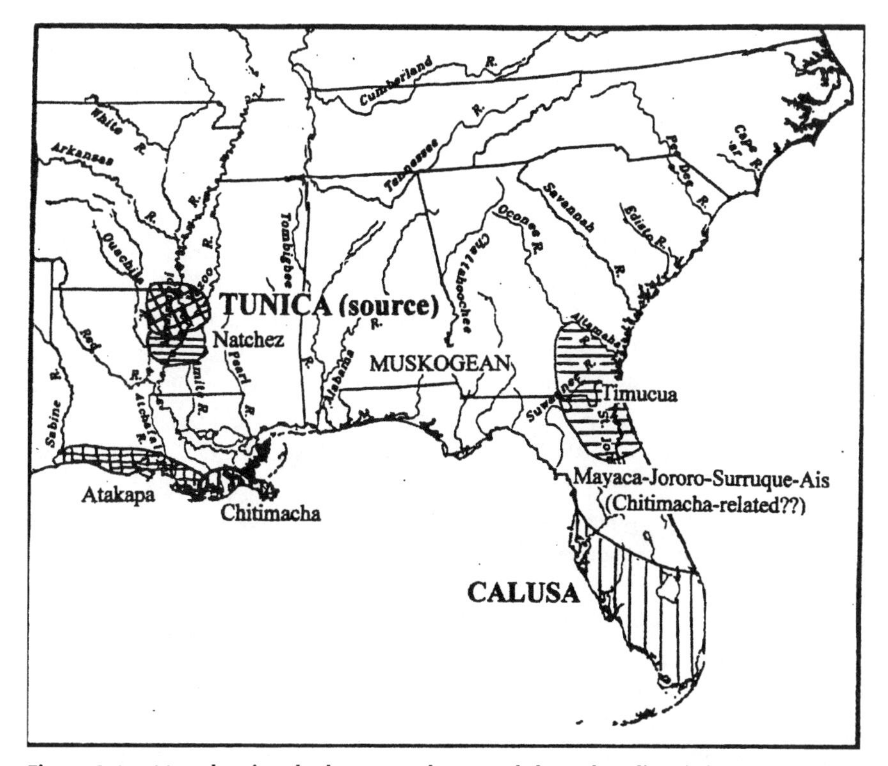

Figure 8.1. Map showing the lower southeast and the Calusa linguistic sources. From Julian Granberry, published in *The Calusa: Linguistic and Cultural Origins and Relationships,* The University of Alabama Press, 2011, p. 9.

While very premature, Byers's complementary autonomous cult kinship members routinely traveled to joint ceremonial sites from their homes. All Woodland Indians, they must have been able to communicate. The idea of transregional, transcultural exchanges of a religious cult, along with trade, is an intriguing subject for further research.

Regarding the people and cultures north of the Calusa, Granberry concludes that the Timucua in the St. Johns River area were linguistically distinctive and connected culturally by origins to the coastal people, from the Archaic into the Woodland periods, who settled in South Carolina and Georgia. Those in the north central and northwestern were Muskogean. Based on Escalante Fontaneda's records, again from the sixteenth century, Granberry has Calusa being spoken up to the Big Bend on the Gulf Coast as well as the Tocobaga on Tampa Bay at Safety Harbor. Is it an accident that the large, nonceramic area of Florida has been independently theorized by Granberry as linguistically homogeneous? The many centuries in North America before the arrival of Europeans on the continent were a dynamic time when existing tribes and much of their autonomy became incorporated into larger cultural identities via new and dominant religious rites and belief systems. What occurred in the east and midwestern portions of the continent mirrored the phenomena that was the Fertile Crescent sixty centuries earlier. The largest in terms of populations as satellite centers was the Mississippi culture in 800 AD to 1600 AD, which were concentrated along the long-established north-south and east-west Mississippi River trade routes. As stated before, the movement toward agriculture and permanent settlements was a radical shift from the centuries-old hunter-gatherer bands and tribes, each with their own areas, beliefs, and clan affiliations. Lithic artifacts all have footprints, and we know that these and probably many resources traveled great distances. I contend that Poverty Point played a significant role in the mound-building epoch in North America. We know from the record that long before Poverty Point was being built in 1650 BC the indigenous people of the continent had long-established land and water routes. Consider now that when you locate Gibson's Poverty Point on a map, the site is eight hundred miles from Thompson and Pluckhahn's Fort Center site, the Great Circle dating 800 BC. If you travel by sea, the Yucatan Peninsula is eight hundred miles away, and eight hundred miles to the northeast you have Byers's beginnings of the Hopewell Mounds in Ohio. Therefore, it is possible to begin to view the Mayaimi and the Calusa in relationship to a broader regional mound-building, each with some shared beliefs and even some common languages.

In terms of the lower southeastern portion of the larger culture region, South Florida was distinctive in its remoteness. The end of the continent beliefs, technologies, and strategies took much longer to arrive, and conversely,

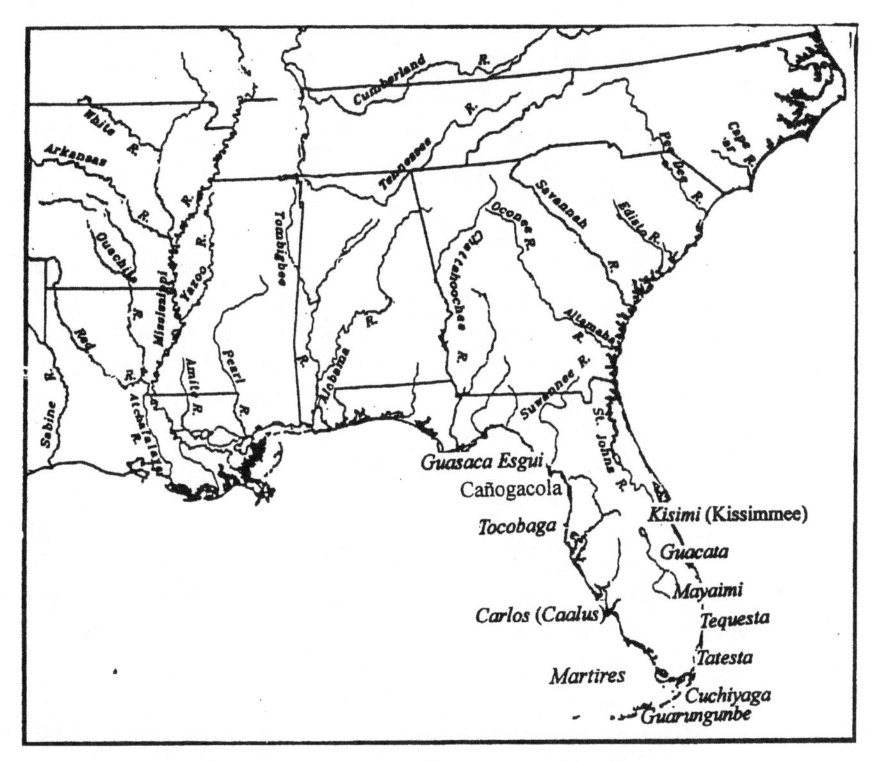

Figure 8.2. Map of the Calusa towns in the 1600s based on the memoirs of Escalante Fontaneda. From Julian Granberry, published in *The Calusa: Linguistic and Cultural Origins and Relationships*, The University of Alabama Press, 2011, p. 9.

those exported took greater time reaching other cultures in North America. Therefore, the Calusa and Mayaimi would have greater contact with the other groups in the Florida peninsula.

In this chapter I will attempt to discuss the chiefdoms of the Calusa and Mayaimi in relationship to the seven other culture regions and chiefdoms that coexisted with them for the majority of the same centuries. To underscore the significance of geography for retaining power and culture in Florida, only two chiefdoms of the eight, both bordering large Mississippi centers, bought completely into their ways. By this I mean centralization of all power.

As I discussed in chapter 3, Jerald Milanich stated that during that period, South Florida consisted of three culture regions: Lake Okeechobee, Caloosahatchee, and Glade. While perhaps a convenient model, there is absolutely little support for these three culture regions. The archaeology of the Everglades and Ten Thousand Islands clearly shows Calusa (Caloosahatchee) and

Glade (Mayaimi) and Teqesta elements. Perfect examples are the mounds and the system of canals at Bear Mound and Mud Lake sites in the extreme southern tip of the peninsula. What he and others classify as Belle Glades and Glade ceramics (now known to be produced elsewhere) were in fact what anthropologists relied on for determining both the extent of the regions or region, as well as their beginning and end dates. Differences in the subsistence pattern because of the similar environments usually produce similar cultural expressions. In fact, that has been the argument now for decades by the archaeological brain trust in Gainesville. The anthropologists spent more time researching the northern cultures that has produced ethnographies not found in the south. If in fact Lake Okeechobee was twice its present size, the region he and others assigned to either the Okeechobee cultural region or the Glade region (never Mayaimi region), that culture would have always been underwater. Milanich and his colleagues have had no problem viewing the Weeden Island culture that had diverse environments and which, at its cultural summit, encompassed over a third of the Florida peninsula as a single culture region. I fail to understand why the same could not have resulted in the southern portion of Florida.

My research supports a theory of a single cultural region in South Florida. The Calusa and Mayaimi leadership and chiefdoms were influential in the largest culture regions that occupied the Florida peninsula from approximately 800 BC to 1700 AD. Typically, such a vast region of approximately twenty thousand square miles would be impossible to maintain and control centrally. I believe there is strong evidence that the Calusa and all of the South Florida culture region was a mixed system combining elements of hunter-gatherer egalitarian social organization mixed with elements of hierarchical complex chiefdoms and social organization. Evidence for this theory can be found in the burial mounds and ceremonial complexes that reveal the coexistence of these two types of organization in the same region over time.

Regarding just how many settlements, villages, and people over time the region possessed, there have been no attempts to speculate. From Escalante Fontaneda we can theorize from his list of Calusa "towns" (figure 8.2). Milanich has speculated that there were hundreds of thousands of natives in Florida by 1492. My request for the number of interior sites in parts of South Florida showed over 1,000. Add the known larger towns on the coasts and you can speculate fifty thousand to one hundred thousand in the southern region around 1450 AD. Other indicators of large populations are the four large regional ceremonial complexes: Fort Center, Ortona, Big Mound City, and Big Circle Mound, unique to South Florida, that were built to accommodate thousands of people at one time. We do know that in the northern portion of the region, the large earthworks and canals at Ortona requiring many people, occurred around 550 to 800 AD. Fort Center just south of Ortona showed increased use and growth during the same timeframe. The new carbon dates for the construction of the Great Circle and the mortuary mound and pond indicate that populations increased and prospered as early as 800 BC. We know that the two neighboring chiefdoms to the north established themselves during the same time in 950 BC: the St. Johns culture northeast and the Deptford culture in the northwest.

When Gordon Willey published the complete taxonomy and chronology for the Florida Gulf Coast, he was careful to characterize the finds from the first forty years of professional excavations. Reviewing the data, he listed the ceramics and their frequency. We had a fairly complete picture of interregional trade spanning twenty-two centuries. In short, as soon as Deptford-style ceramics showed up, they were also found in the other two regions. The same went for St. Johns ceramics found in large quantities and very early in the Okeechobee region. My connecting of Milner's periods of war and peace helps to understand why chiefdoms increased or decreased contact and trade during specific periods. One culture region was in continuous interaction with them during the entire epoch, the St. Johns River region.

The chiefdoms in the northeast adjoining the Calusa and Mayaimi, identified as the St. Johns River culture, were the tribe and chiefdom of the Timucua people. Their center was inland from the Atlantic coast on islands above the St. Johns River estuary. They were a classic riverine culture that transitioned from Archaic period settlements that established themselves over the entire southeast region of North America. Like their neighbors they took advantage of interior hunting lands, shellfish in the estuary, and coastal fish and shell resources. Based on the archaeological record, the lands of the Timucua in Florida were approximately ten thousand square miles. Unlike the Mayaimi people, we know a great deal about this culture. As I stated in chapter 1, ceramics is and has been the focus of Florida archaeology, and the St. Johns River region had a rich ceramic tradition. Even today, kaolin clays are mined in Putnam County and exported for use in fine porcelain. Their ancestors in southern Georgia were the first to manufacture ceramics in North America in the Late Archaic period around 2500 BC. When you look at the map created by the Florida Geological Survey (figure 4.1) in chapter 4, you see they had both eastern and western sources of clay, while the south had none. The Timucua also benefited by their lands being close to the rich Atlantic coastal trade routes in the southeastern United States. Unlike the Mayaimi and Calusa, they were close to exotic materials such as rocks and minerals traded out of Georgia. Having a desirable pottery to trade as well as shells for tools and ornaments, the Timucua were trade rich. Their ceramics have been found all over the central and southern areas, revealing that both areas had good relationships and a persistent alliance. The geography and the trade routes also, as I pointed out in chapter 3, made the Timucua vulnerable to attacks. The accounts by the Spanish indicate that wars were constant in the region, and the Timucua had a strong warrior class as a result. My research indicates, however, that there have been no accounts of skeletal remains, especially those that indicate death from violence and warfare in this important culture region.

The discovery of shell rings in the St. Johns areas gives us insight into their beliefs and ways. The building of shell rings for ritual landscapes connects them or their ancestors to a broad belief culture that was prevalent globally and preceded mound-building during the Neolithic period. These early ceremonial earthworks were rarely found with agriculture but rather mark the earliest religious expressions of settled egalitarian hunter-gathering societies. Shell rings have been found north of the St. Johns River on coastal islands and river estuaries in Georgia and South Carolina. As I discussed in chapter 3, shell ring ritual spaces were built during long and pronounced periods of violence and warfare. The presence of St. Johns ceramics throughout South Florida is a clear indicator that both culture areas lived peacefully with each other.

The Timucua were part of the mound-building cultural epoch in the Southeastern region. The history shows that mound-building played a much less cultural role as compared with their neighbors. They did build one immense mound that the public can still view—Turtle Mound—that is now in the protected Cape Canaveral National Seashore Park (figure 8.3). It was built the same time as the Great Serpent Mound in Ohio around 1000 AD. One cannot but wonder if the mound shape and location were an attempt to reference the Turtle Island origins myth. Turtle Mound, as a major project of a ceremonial mound, underscores that they were a hunter-gatherer, egalitarian style of social organization. On my proposed Florida taxonomy chart, I have them mixed during the St. Johns II period. Milanich writes that after 1050 AD, they adopted the domestication of plants, and populations in the central to lower portions of the region faced large population growth. For a brief period, the lower settlements went the complex social organizational route and adopted strong chiefdoms. Therefore, for a period they were mixed, having both types of social-political organization.

Based on my research and reevaluation of the culture regions and chronologies, there is evidence to suggest that these more complex communities were actually Safety Harbor variants of the Calusa and Glade cultures. This area would have been vital to maintaining the Atlantic coastal trade.

The St. Johns River region shared its rich Archaic period with the cultures in the south. Both regions buried their dead in shallow freshwater ponds, marshes, or springs. Finds such as the Windover Pond site near Titusville, Florida, show a large bog burial site dating back to 6000 to 5000 BC. The mummified, prepared water burials indicated a rich, woven cloth tradition and

Figure 8.3. Turtle Mound, New Smyma Beach, Florida, built by the Timucua people, is clearly visible from the Atlantic Ocean. The mound contains over 35,000 cubic yards of shells and was originally 600 feet long by 50 feet high. The Florida Department of State, Florida Memories.

technology. Water burials are rare in North America. During the same period, other societies performed water burials in the Southwest in Sarasota County at Little Salt Springs and Warm Mineral Springs. The newest site was found in 2016, three hundred feet offshore of Manasota Key under twenty feet of water. The Offshore Manasota Key site contained over one hundred individuals buried in a freshwater pond and preserved by peat in 5000 BC.

Figure 8.4. *Hontoon Owl,* carved wooden owl effigy found on Hontoon Island, St. Johns River, Florida.

To conclude, the St. Johns culture dates back to the late Archaic period in Florida. It was one of three major cultures that continued as regional cultures into the Woodland periods. All three had long-established histories that included trading because of the origins of and geographical location of the St. Johns people. The southern cultures had to rely on trade with the St. Johns people for ceramics, as well as exotic mineral resources, resources so important that they could not risk an unfavorable relationship.

The Northwest central peninsula neighboring chiefdoms were much different culturally when compared to the south. Take, for example, the many subregional chiefdoms of the Weeden Island culture. The Weeden Island culture was defined and classified very early in the twentieth century. It remains the most researched regional culture in Florida. Compared with the south, Weeden was another distinctly northern culture. My views on the Weeden have altered dramatically because of my ceramic findings. There are many different theories about the Weeden Island culture. We know of them primarily because of their decorative pottery (figure 8.5). You could say the Weeden people were the opposites of the Calusa. They had multiple sources of clay, and not only produced everyday ceramic vessels but also a distinctive and imaginative, highly decorated "sacred" style of ceramic vessels. Comparing the exquisite nonceramic artifacts of the Calusa, the Calusa engineering skills, along with the ritual centers of the Mayaimi, they were worlds apart. The Weeden culture has been dated from 200 AD to 1200 AD. While a decent amount of time, the cultures in the south existed 1,500 years longer. I attribute this shorter duration to three factors. First, the territory of the Weeden people in North Central Florida had them boxed in. They had competing and nonalliance cultures on both sides. Based on the archaeological records, the beliefs, ways, and customs of the Weeden people did not bode well with their neighbors. With the exception of the western Gulf coastal people from Pasco County to Tampa Bay, Weeden ceramics are never recovered. The second reason is that they do not appear to have worked out a successful organizational strategy. They had certain villages with strong chiefs who competed with other villages with strong chiefs. These were interspersed with transient and mostly settled groups and villages of egalitarian-style hunter-gatherers. It is apparent from the archaeology that the primary Weeden Island group migrated from central Georgia. One could theorize that such a migration gave them the advantage of having access to a portion of the Gulf Coast not controlled by other groups, which gave them the food and freshwater resources of the interior and the marine resources of the Gulf of Mexico. Now as late as 200 AD the river estuaries and the coastal bays would have been very populated. Therefore, they negotiated with the locals. They more than likely continued such negotiations, successfully and unsuccessfully, for one thousand years. The

Figure 8.5. Drawings of Weeden Island ceramics. From Gordon R. Willey's *Archaeology of the Florida Gulf Coast*, The Smithsonian Institution, 1949.

Calusa were newcomers. When they migrated to southwest Florida, there were many indigenous people who had lived in the area for thousands of years. They too ended up with a mixed type of social organization, but one that withstood the ravages of time. The third reason for the rise and fall of the Weeden was their beliefs. Returning to Martin Byers, you do not find the multiple-mound complexes or multiuse mortuary/mound complexes in the Weeden culture area. This indicates to me that despite the appearance of Hopewellian influences, they did not have cult affiliates. It is like saying you will not find local lodges of the Elks. These cult kinship groups, remember, were entrusted with maintaining the balance between the two-legged and the four-legged, the maintaining of the purity of the land and the people. Archaeologists have brought attention to the Weeden culture's view of animals, a view in which humans ranked much higher—the complete opposite view of the Calusa and Mayaimi, which I will discuss in chapter 9.

As I stated at the beginning, my views of the Weeden culture changed after my research proved that that large area of the western Gulf Coast, always considered Weeden, and in fact gave the culture its name, had no clay. It is one thing to be an active cultural area, and quite another to import your ceramics from another culture. Considering the hodgepodge of Weeden politics and social organization, I have theorized that with this large area from Tampa Bay north, the Weeden Island territorial boundaries would have been too vast to organize and maintain. This had to be the case, especially considering the vast number of dedicated egalitarian fishing-hunter-gathering groups.

The archaeology shows that the South actually advanced and came together as a culture, based on the new dates for the Great Circle, a full one thousand years before the earliest Weeden sites dated 200 AD. It has been commonly believed that over centuries, the Weeden Island culture had a territory much larger than that of the Calusa, Mayaimi, and Tequesta cultures, approximately twenty thousand square miles. The Weeden Island culture's influence and reputation extended far beyond its territories for a brief period. Because of their size and a natural tendency for each culture to expand and particularly control the rich coastal waters along the west coast, warfare persisted between chiefs from both regions from approximately 400 AD to 1200 AD. Granberry's research emphasized the importance of the long-established Gulf Coast corridor. As warfare increased after 400 AD, the Weeden chiefs controlled the important northern and northwestern trade corridor and had that distinctive advantage for a good eight hundred years. The lessons of this prehistoric epoch were that the real power was in the religious beliefs. Nowhere in the Weeden Island region are there multi-mound ceremonial complexes, like those found in the South. A collection of great circular centers does not appear in the Weeden culture regions, once centered in the Cedar Keys region in the coastal bays at the mouth of the Suwannee River in Levy County, and over time extended westward and southward. On a map from Fontaneda's memoirs, he noted two Calusa towns, Guasaca Esqui and Caflogacob. Anthropologists (figure 8.2) have never mentioned this anomaly in any of their investigations of the region. The Safety Harbor site is also shown on Escalante Fontaneda's map and referred to as the town called Tocobaga.

While yet investigated, this primary source indicates a later influx of the South Florida culture into Central Florida after the demise of the Weeden after 1200 AD. Weeden chiefs had lost ground in the battle for the hearts and souls of its people.

William Sears and later Randolph Widmer referred to the Glade III period in South Florida as a period marked by a decrease of decorative ceramics, and a period lacking ceramics produced by the cultures of the northwest regions. There is ample evidence that the Weeden interrupted north-south trade for many centuries. It is also an archaeological fact that no Weeden ceramics were ever found below the Tampa Bay area, and even there they found very few, because nature abhors vacuums and supercharged Mississippian cultures like the Fort Walton people and the Safety Harbor people took hold in their territories. One thing is abundantly clear from the archaeological record, and this is opposite the views of Milanich and others who have written on the subject. Further proof of the decline of the Weeden culture was a Levy County site discussed in Willey's compilation. The Palmetto Island archaeologists found that the greater number of ceramic artifacts were St. Johns types from the northeastern region of Florida, mainly used in the burials of their leaders and social elites. There were little variations in their villages. Weeden life, it appears, was heavily regulated and ordered. Ritual space was structured for viewing. Unlike the communal and participatory spaces in the south, the ritual spaces were associated with each village and the social ranking of the chief or the strong man. Temple mounds with public plazas, not found in the south until after 1200 AD, were everywhere in the north-central region. For all intents and purposes, the Weeden was a characteristic feudal society.

Before the arrival of the Calusa, and about the same time of the Mayaimi in the south, the earliest expression of the Weeden epoch, the Deptford, made the northwest areas their home around 1000 BC. The Deptford evolved into the Swift Creek during the period of peace and the arrival of the Calusa. Their region was always a Gulf coastal and interior river culture, not at all different from their neighboring regions. By alliance, cooperation and survival hunter and photorealists in the interior managed their resources and futures with the marine-rich coastal peoples. Beliefs were the critical agents to social unity, order, and continuity.

Before the mound-builders, before the arrival of the Calusa and the Weeden people, annual feasting along the coast was the important strategy for social organization and cohesion. I liken the coastal areas in Florida during the millenniums before the birth of Christ as not unlike the northwest coastal communities. Feasts or potlatches were events for the cycles of life. The centers that the Calusa and Weeden people discovered were built by autonomous clans that were affiliated and very mobile inhabitants. These centers were characterized by burial mounds connected to large shell rings. Sites such as Perico Island in Manatee County, the Palmer site in Sarasota County, and the Goodland site in Collier County are the vestiges of the transitional stage before the mounds. It is important to know that especially in the central and southern regions of the Florida peninsula that these earlier ways existed late into the mound-building phases. That they coexisted side-by-side with the newer forms that immigrated into the area 500 BC to 500 AD gives a more complete picture of Florida prehistory. Similar to Europe during the Early Middle Ages, the ability of the leaders of the new beliefs and ways to work with the indigenous inhabitants was critical for social cohesion and peace.

Returning to a discussion of the other cultures and their regions during the Woodland periods, west of the Weeden people in the Florida panhandle were the Swift Creek and Santa Rosa. Again, identified by archaeologists primarily for the ceramic types, the Swift Creek evolved out of the Deptford, and so they were a Florida expression of a large cultural sphere that encompassed lower Georgia, Alabama, and Mississippi. The timing of their culture, with an increase in social complexity and ceremonialism, corresponds with the beginnings of the Hopewell culture in Ohio and the spread of Hopewellian influence on the hunter-gathering societies of the Woodland period around 200 AD. Santa Rosa, a later version that had increased sites around Pensacola, had obvious origins, demonstrated in their ceramics to the Marksville culture. The geographical size and limits of both the Swift Creek and Santa Rosa was about ten thousand miles. The archaeological records do not show a great deal of contact and trade with the cultures on the peninsula and the south. Some archaeologists believe that they were culturally connected to the Weeden Island culture, but my research indicates that the two cultures were often adversarial, owing to competing interest, beliefs, and different kinship groups and alliances.

Just east in northwestern Florida, and much later, the Fort Walton culture developed and occupied the rich Gulf coastal area from 1200 to 1500. Fort Walton was a fully expressed Mississippi culture in northern Florida. Fort Walton was contemporary with Cahokia, the great mound complex on the Mississippi River, built during the cultural zenith of the Mississippi people 1050 to 1350 AD. The Lake Jackson, Fort Walton site built on a lake north of Tallahassee is the largest ceremonial complex in northern Florida. Now a state archaeological park, Lake Jackson is made up of seven mounds. By comparison, Fort Center in the south, completed centuries earlier, had sixteen mounds. There is much evidence of exchange between Fort Walton and the southern culture region during their brief three-hundred-year period.

The Alachua culture occupied a small slice of the interior of north-central Marion and Putnam counties. Archaeologists who have studied the Alachua have more questions than answers. For one, they were cultivators of maize. They actually used corn cobs to texture their pottery. Second, they settled entirely in hardwood hammocks, interior marsh areas with no coastal territory. In many ways, they were like the Mayaimi, except for the maize and some of the most abundant clay sources. They made superior ceramics, probably due to their origins in the Piedmont or coastal areas of Georgia. Interesting was their dates of occupation, from 600 to 1700 AD. The neighboring St. Johns culture to the east was established over a millennium before their arrival, and likewise the Weeden culture to the west were occupying their lands eight hundred years prior. The Alachua people occupied the exact lands of the Cades Pond culture. Therefore, there is something akin to an ecological niche in play.

The last of the neighboring cultures was the Safety Harbor culture. Identified early by archaeologists primarily by their decorative ceramics, from the time of Gordon Willey and John Goggin, researchers believed that the Safety Harbor culture took hold rather late in Florida prehistory. Like their namesake, a small, hilly area with a well-known spring, Safety Harbor overlooks the Tampa Bay. The frequency of excavated Safety Harbor ceramic vessels in the counties surrounding Tampa Bay, they all assumed that they were a Tampa Bay area culture. My research has resulted in a very different view. In 1989, Jeffrey McClain Mitchem, while a graduate student, wrote a dissertation titled *Redefining Safety Harbor*. Mitchem believed that his research not only established them as a major culture but also claimed they had a much larger culture region and three distinctive chronologic periods. Even after reviewing his research, I could not stop thinking about Escalante Fontaneda's claim of Safety Harbor being a major Calusa town in the early 1500s. As I stated earlier, two other Calusa towns mentioned were in the previous Weeden region, way up the western Gulf Coast. Mitchem claimed that that area later was Safety Harbor.

Common sense made me question that the arrival of a totally new culture can be first recognized by Englewood ceramics in southern Sarasota County around 900 AD. Willey and the established view in the mid-twentieth century was that Weeden Island occupied the entire western Gulf Coast from 1000 to 1500 AD. Then Fort Walton took the northern territories and Safety Harbor, the southern territories of the Weeden culture. Fort Walton, as I explained, was a later expression of Santa Rosa. Logically because the Calusa controlled the entire southern region by 1000 AD, Safety Harbor would have been a regional variance of Calusa. Here, I return to Randolph Widmer. Widmer on page 86 of *The Evolution of the Calusa* wrote:

> Bullen (1978:50) has suggested that the Safety Harbor Phase is the archaeological manifestation of the ethnographic group the Tocobaga. This is partly accurate, but this phase, as represented in the ceramics, is not

> isomorphic with the Tocobaga, particularly since Safety Harbor ceramics extend geographically into the Charlotte Harbor area (Bullen 1969:418), which is the heartland of the Calusa (Goggin and Sturtevant 1964). . . . A more reasonable interpretation, the one suggested here, is that Safety Harbor material culture is typical of both the Tocobaga and the Calusa.

Widmer goes on to talk about the nondecorative and utilitarian ceramics of the Safety Harbor culture, which are indistinguishable with those used by the Calusa, Glade Plain ceramics. When you include my discovery that no class existed in the Safety Harbor region, except for Polk County, then it seems likely that the Safety Harbor and the Calusa both imported ceramics, and probably from the same neighboring region.

Jeffrey Mitchem inadvertently helped to support a conflicting view by using certain burial mounds in support of a separate and distinctive Safety Harbor culture. First, the Philip Mound in Polk County, which had a large quantity of Belle Glade and Glade ceramics, prove that essentially that Safety Harbor was a variant and culturally connected to the south. The very distinctive Thomas Mound in Manatee County, when Clarence B. Moore first excavated, had a characteristically Calusa canal going from its base to the river. Finally, numerous metal tablets with Calusa symbols have been excavated from Safety Harbor sites (figure 8.6). The most recent was found by George Luer in downtown Tampa. Coincidence? I doubt it.

Widmer's remarks are in a chapter in which he describes the Caloosahatchee period IV, which he states is marked by an increase in decorative burial ceramics in the south. Remember, most probably the lack of it in prior periods was due to the Weeden disrupting trade. The question then is why the Calusa would allow another competing chiefdom to take over the same territories and threaten the trade once more. That is why I believe that the Safety Harbor peoples were connected and allied with the Calusa. This would assure for generations that Calusa had control of all north-south trade routes. This hypothesis is totally supported by the artifacts, the material record 900 AD to 1700 AD.

A testimony to the unique cultural differences, north to south, is that the Mississippi expressions in the north reached their zenith in the building of Cahokia on the Mississippi near present-day St. Louis. It was a heavily fortified urban center, agriculturally based with evidence of large numbers of human sacrifices and rigid social controls. Around Lake Okeechobee, at that time and centuries later, there were no such aberrations. For all intents and purposes, they had held to their cherished beliefs and ways of life.

In my introduction, I told of my interactions with the last hunter-gatherers in the then Soviet Union. I delivered a presentation to the conference on bio-regionalism, a view of sustainable living comparable to the early

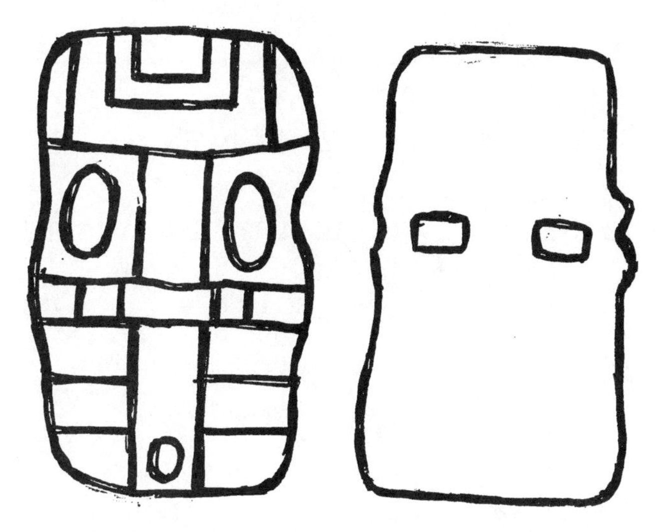

Figure 8.6. Drawing of Calusa-inspired metal tablet found at the Thomas Mound in Hillsborough County. Gordon R. Willey, *Archaeology of the Florida Gulf Coast,* The Smithsonian Institution, 1949.

hunter-gathering societies. My translator struggled for a translation in Russian for bio-regionalism. We agreed upon "region full of life." It probably should have been "living region," since all regions contain life. South Florida after the last Ice Age was a region full of life. It was truly the land of milk and honey if you could adapt to it. The Spaniards saw the region in terms of what it lacked. In terms of white settlers, it was their last choice; a proper viewing of the Calusa, Mayaimi, and Tequesta people in their local context was an environment with more than enough and far away enough to let them be.

• 9 •

Some Totally Unique Cultural Variations

> We conclude that the southern Florida region in general represents one of the most extensively constructed built environments by hunter-gatherers in world prehistory.
>
> —Victor D. Thompson and Thomas J. Pluckhahn, *New Histories of Precolumbian Florida*

> Not unfrequently there occur in these fens, which contain the largest and highest islands the so-called hammocks which in the main are but ancient settlements and owe their present height to accumulations of soil brought there laboriously by the Indians.
>
> —Frank Hamilton Cushing, *The Lost Manuscripts of Frank Hamilton Cushing*

The Calusa were one of only a few people in human history to choose to live and thrive, as well as have dominion, over an archipelago. Anthropologists have known from day one that culture is the specific adaptation by humans to specific places. The Great Charlotte Harbor, Pine Island Sound, Bonito Bay, and Ten Thousand Island areas of southwest Florida is such an archipelago. Cushing reported early on in the Pepper-Hearst expedition that many of the islands and keys were man made. Recent archeology in the Pacific, specifically pertaining to the island of Pohnpei, a part of a greater Micronesian archipelago, reveals the same practice. Not only were the ancient inhabitants creating and joining islands, like the Calusa in Florida, they were engineering canals and canal systems. When I think of the Pacific Islands, I think of their incredible wood carvings. When I study the wood carvings of the Calusa, especially the mechanical deer, wolf, and crane carved ceremonial headpieces with movable parts, I think of the wood-carving tradition of another archipelago on the northwest coast of North America. I envision the great fishing-hunter-gatherers in their large, decorated dugout canoes. I can imagine the rich tradition of costumed storytelling at great gatherings, and the incredible feasts given and received.

A secondary meaning to the word *archipelago* is "scattered." What I personally view as the exceptional work of the Calusa in Florida is the organic and scattered placement of houses, ceremonial mounds, burial mounds, ponds, and canals. In the visual arts we refer to this style of design as asymmetrical. When you compare all Calusa complexes to other important complexes in North America, they are unique in their scatterings. Poverty Point in Louisiana is beautifully symmetrical, classical, and in the order of ancient Greek and Roman works. The Calusa encountered and soon made a long and fruitful alliance with the Lake People of the interior. They viewed the cosmos as ordered and symmetrical, and they used the unifying and complete symbol of the circle in their ceremonial centers. Opposites don't always attract when it comes to cultural alliances, but in Florida they did. They went so far as to merge their cultures and beliefs, creating something unique, human, and sustainable.

If the Calusa world was an island oasis in the deep coastal salt waters of the Gulf, the world of the Lake People was an inland sea of shallow freshwater lakes and swamps. Their oasis, and there was oasis, were hammocks protected by great trees and palmettos and tree islands supported all the two-legged inhabitants of water world (figure 9.1). Cushing never visited this watery interior, but he spent pages aptly describing the environment in the first pages of his Florida manuscript. In the decades to come, it is these interior islands that would yield some of the most significant archaeological finds in North American prehistory—a reason for my rebuttal to Milanich's assertion that the lifeways of the south were no different from the north of Florida. Even in the nineteenth century, Native Americans flourished in the southern region that white settlers found difficult to impossible. In contrast, aboriginal people considered the lands to be sacred, and it once was a spiritual center for thousands of resourceful and expressive inhabitants.

Unique also was that the region was not on the way to somewhere else. They did not have regular flights or cruises out of Miami. Going great distances in dugout canoes to the islands and South America was not favored. That means the cultures in South Florida had far less contact with other cultures. They grew and developed independently, and that independent nature stayed as a prominent characteristic to the end. The geography of southern Florida favored the eventual probability, not inevitability, of difference from their neighbors further north.

Figure 9.1. Photograph of tree islands in the northern Everglades.

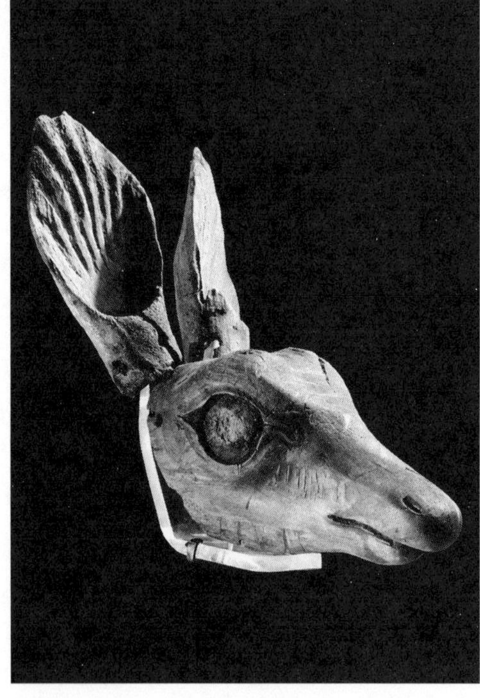

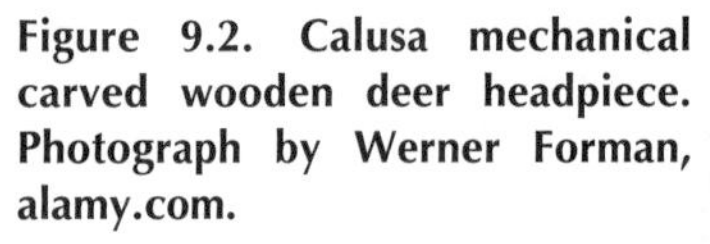

Figure 9.2. Calusa mechanical carved wooden deer headpiece. Photograph by Werner Forman, alamy.com.

Figure 9.3. Watercolor of Calusa mask found at Key Marco, 1896.

The big picture of the Calusa and their neighbors indicating and supporting the view of their uniqueness was their strong sense of self-identity, confidence in their beliefs, and their skills. No other group of Woodland period mound-builders built systems of canals. No other Woodland period mound-builders created great circular ceremonial centers dug deep in the mother earth to reestablish the unity of all life. No group lasted as long as the Calusa and their neighbors. They did all this and more without agriculture and the conventional making and use of pottery. In terms of the artifacts left behind, the clues as to who they were as a people are to be found in emblems made from metal, stone, and wood. For the sacred in fashioned articles by the Calusa, you must look to their wood carvings.

What first drew me to these prehistoric dwellers, as stated in my introduction, were the wood carvings. William Marquardt in his *The Calusa and Their Legacy* book recognized the "excellence" and distinctiveness of Calusa wood carvings. He then writes only four sentences contradicting this view in lacking support. Yet in his *The Archaeology of Pineland*, Marquardt dedicates an entire chapter to the "mechanical" crane headpiece, comparing it to the only similar wood carvings similar in North America, the Northwest Coast tribes. The three-dimensional and relief carvings of birds, reptiles, animals, and humans are naturalistic in style. By that I mean that the contours and proportions match those actually found in nature. No other native artists in the world at this time employed this style (figure 9.2). Even Marquardt, when discussing the crane headpiece found at Pine Island, stated:

> The Thomasson bird artifact is natural in form, apparently lacking stylized abstractions, and probably was intended by its creator to represent a natural species.

For instance, when you look at the wood-carving tradition of the Northwest Coast, birds, animals, and humans are depicted in highly abstracted contours, lines, and shapes. Like the contemporaries in the South Pacific region, there were no attempts to mirror the natural world. That is because they were depicting spiritual beings. Power animals and totem animals were preserved as supernatural. This brings us to one of the unique variants found in the Calusa material culture. Sears in Fort Center remarked about the multitude of the bird and animal carvings found at the mortuary site that most probably were clan totems. Clans were at the time systems used to unify the growing tribal populations by creating subgroups. This long socioeconomic and political system using totem animals was important. Sears, while acknowledging that the hundreds of carvings were probably totems, then stated he didn't believe they had any importance to the community. Despite this view, he hired artists to carefully recreate each bird or beast effigy as if it were newly carved, a before-disintegration-and-centuries-of-decay view. When you look at these images of the pantheon of birds and beasts, they are inescapably Calusa. The originals, as with all Calusa carvings, were painted, making them less naturalistic but more impressive. But these representations are a unique variant because they are not known clan totems. For instance, many species of cat and dogs were found. If you do your homework, you realize that there were never any dog or cat clans. The question then arises: If they were not totems, what were they, and what function did they serve?

Masks worn by performers, storytellers, and shaman can be found around the world. They speak to the humanity of these ancient people, as well as their sense and belief of identity. Again, the Calusa painted and carved masks were both numerous and expressive (figure 9.3). They were unfortunately the first to deteriorate when they were removed by the protective muck at the Key Marco site. The large number of masks and other ritual and ceremonial artifacts excavated at the Key Marco site in 1896 led Cushing to believe that the location played a significant role in regional ritual and ceremony.

I contend that the presence of so many naturalistic and species-specific carvings was the full expression of the religious beliefs and ways of the people. This view was made and argued by Wheeler in his 2000 *Treasure of the Calusa*. The Calusa and the Lake People viewed all life, including humans, in common as one creation—they were animists. This view proceeds beautifully and consistently with their probable origin myths. The Tree of Life gave life to all the creatures, the larger circle consisting of all beings (figure 10.2). All were imbued with spirit. This symbol, which has been unearthed at multiple sites in South Florida, I will discuss fully in the next chapter. The Judeo-Christian genesis story, one of many Neolithic period creation stories, had the definitive agricultural-based twist in which humans only were made in God's image and likeness and given dominion over the beasts and birds. The stories carried down by all of the tribes of North America have references to a grandmother tree, grandmother spider, and so on, indicating the distinctive view of these tribes of common ancestry with and cooperation among all of creation. That is not to say that the Calusa and Mayaimi did not have social stratifications and classes of people, and you were born into positions of authority. They did, but this required stratification was balanced with more feminine organizing principals of cooperation, and they were "fluid." That was the way for millennia with hunter-gatherers. This last until the end again, due to their geographical remoteness, as well as their choice not to transition to agriculturally based cultures.

Another significant variant that has escaped all subsequent anthropological research on the Calusa and Glade since Cushing in 1896 is the incorporation of man-made pools and ponds at all ceremonial mounds and complexes. The fact that this feature is not found at any similar site in North and South America and has received no mention is inexplicable. I can only surmise that just as these same researchers assumed there had to be other great woodcarving cultures without verification, they assumed that many of the other

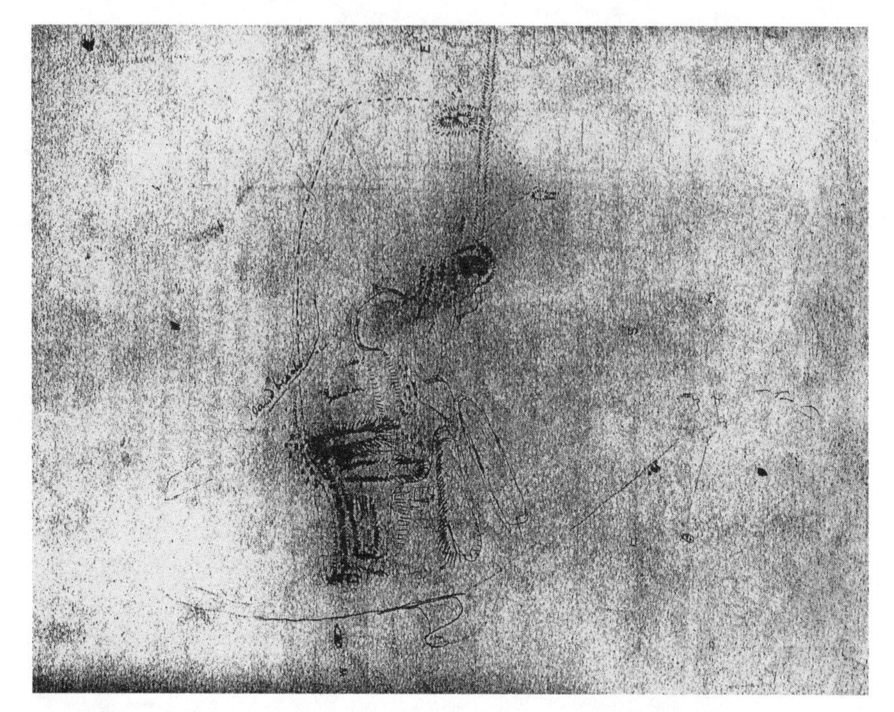

Figure 9.4. Drawing of Battey's Landing, Calusa site, Pine Island. Presently the mound is part of the Randell Research Center. The Culin Archival Collection, The Brooklyn Museum.

mound complexes in North America had ponds and water courts. It cannot be more dramatically clear from Cushing's expedition that every basically undisturbed Calusa mound complex up and down the southern Gulf Coast incorporated a ceremonial pond and/or water court. Cushing referenced such discoveries and drew site maps illustrating this point numerous times (figure 9.4). Key Marco and Fort Center are two known examples of burial mounds with charnel platforms and houses that also had a mortuary pond. It is also a fact that as soon as you travel out of the Calusa kingdom there are no such man-made water features. This is proof positive that what often escapes many anthropologists is the most obvious. Not one author to date has paid any mind to the water courts.

An equally unique variant not found elsewhere were the Calusa systems of canals (figure 9.5). As if the giant mounds of shell and the man-made ponds were not major engineering feats for nonagriculture societies, canals were everywhere in South Florida. Florida archaeologists George Luer and Ryan Wheeler have both researched the cultural phenomena of the canals in South

Figure 9.4B. Archaeological reconstruction of the Big Mound Key site.

Florida. While Luer attributes their engineering to the Calusa, Wheeler insists that they were expressions of many localized subcultures that together made up the Glade complex. In his 1995 article on the canals at the Ortona site in Glades County (figure 9.6), Wheeler has a map showing the wide, geographical locations, east and west coasts, the Everglades, and the interior of canals. Wheeler, impressed with the engineering feat demonstrated by the Calusa-built canal at Mud Lake (figure 9.7), successfully had the site designated as one of the only National Historic Landmarks in Florida.

Unfortunately, the systems of canals were early victims of the development in South Florida by the 1930s. They were even more extensive than even Wheeler realized. The Thomas burial mound complex excavated by Clarence Moore in Hillsborough County had a canal running from the base

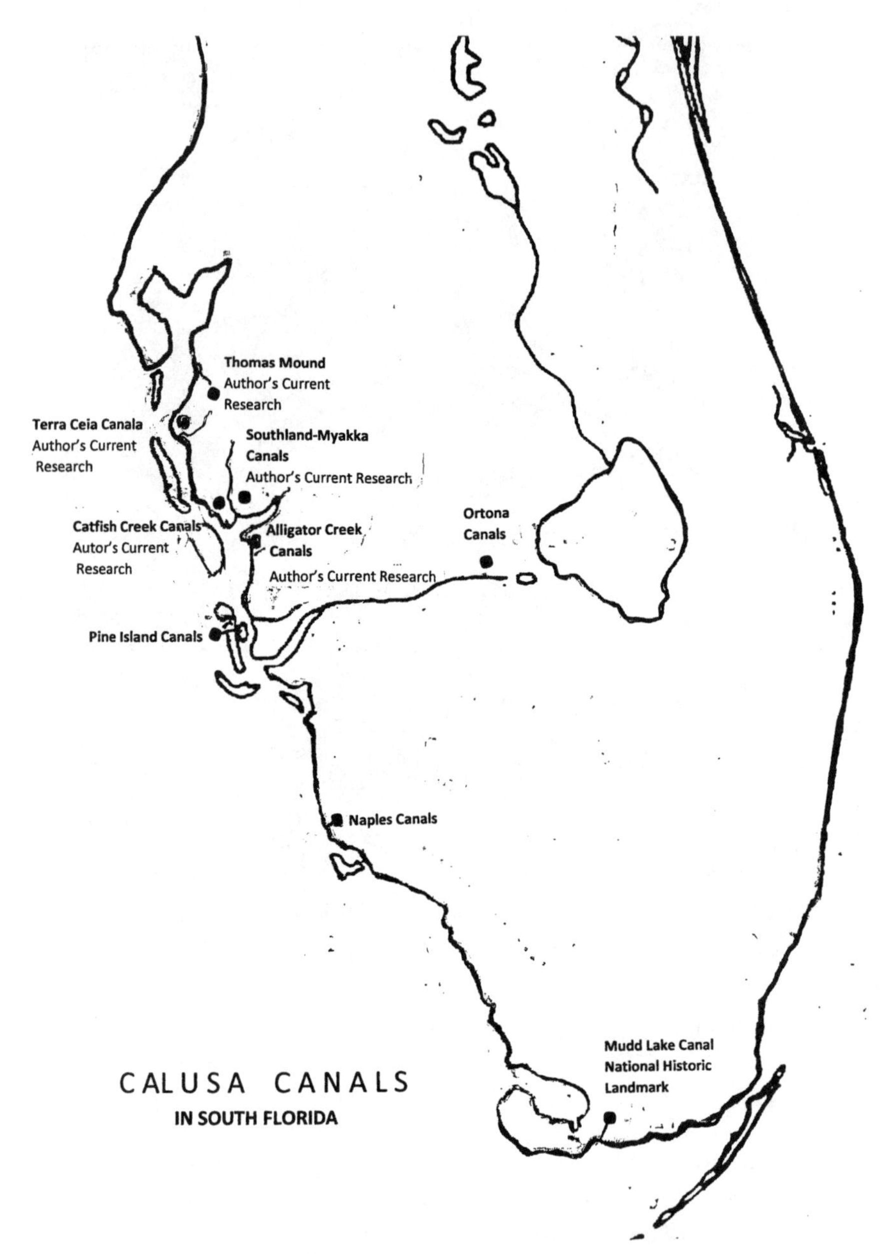

Figure 9.5. Map of the South Florida region showing Calusa-engineered canals. From a map of known canals (1989). George M. Luer with additional canals being researched by the author.

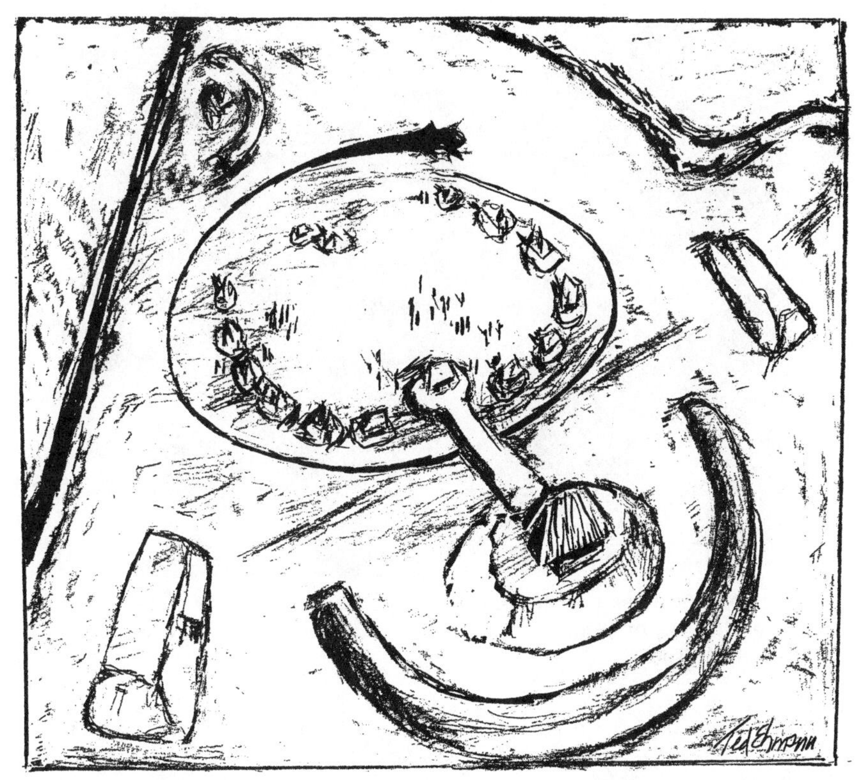

Figure 9.6. Archaeological reconstruction of a portion of the Ortona complex, Ortona, Glades County, Florida. The well-known Calusa engineered canals connect the center below the falls to the Caloosahatchee River. Ted Ehmann, 2019.

of the mound to the water. This past year, using satellite images, I have found what I believe to be systems of canals in the wetland surrounding Charlotte Harbor in Charlotte County and Terra Ceia in Manatee County. Just as the canal reported by Moore at the turn of the century in Hillsborough County, the canals I am researching are all near known burial mounds and Calusa settlements of the thirteenth century. It was exactly like those of the Calusa much further south, as drawn by Cushing in 1896. Willey reports this in his book, as well as its destruction in the 1920s before archaeologists could revisit the site. Using my references in world history, though, it is hard to accept a theory of independently built canals by many tribes in the region. History supports (the Greeks and Romans) a view of one main culture specializing and excelling in such engineering feats. The canals built again by strictly fishing-hunter-gathering people in South Florida was not only unique in the history of aboriginal North America but also in world history. The fact that all the major

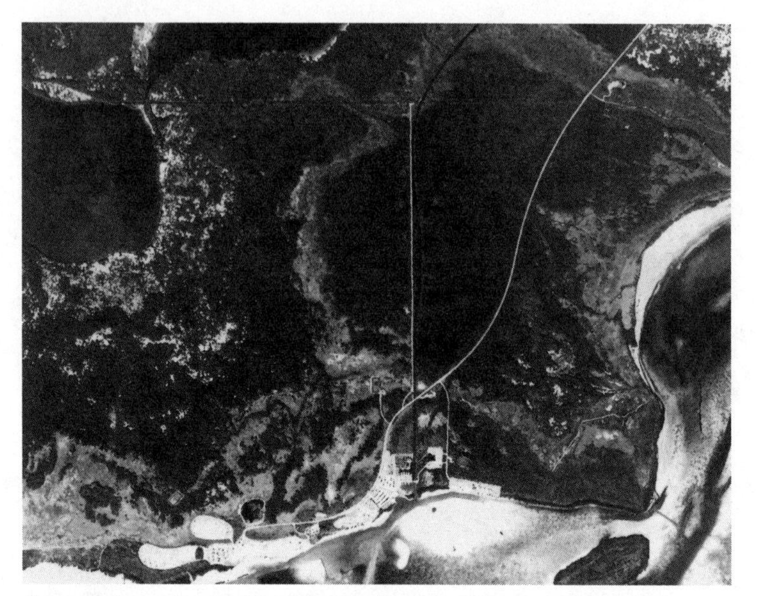

Figure 9.7. Calusa-engineered Mud Lake Canal, Monroe County. The Canal is one of a few National Historic Landmarks in Florida. From wikipedia.com.

contributors (Goggin, Sturtevant, Milanich) completely ignore the phenomena is mind-boggling. Perhaps, they think as I do, that they were clearly the work of the Calusa and as such threatened their sacred Glades theory. Whatever the reasons for their collective avoidance of the subject, who built the canals and why are the most important questions to be researched and answered.

Possible clues might be found in Granberry's linguistic research on the Calusa. If as theorized the Calusa arrived here from the marshes of Louisiana, they may have brought advanced hydraulics and engineering skills from that similar environment. Canals predominate in that region today. Cape Coral that was developed last century in the heart of the Calusa realm is called the Venice of the West. The city is a large system of canals that connect all of its parts with the Gulf of Mexico. When Cushing landed on Pine Island, he was amazed by the deep, wide canals linking the large mound complexes on the western shore clear across the wide island to Matlacha Pass. The canals the Calusa built at the Ortona village (figure 9.6) in the interior near the great lake connected these large, sacred complexes with the river systems to empty near the Calusa capitol. This system was a key component for cultural unity by addressing the need for the transfer of goods and people, as well as a vital communication system. The only other canal system in the new world was later built by the Aztecs, who needed fresh water transported to their saltwater lake capital. How soon anthropologists in South Florida forget, once the great canal systems of the Calusa were bulldozed and built upon. If they accomplished nothing else, those engineering accomplishments were enough to acclaim them as a uniquely distinctive culture.

In chapter 2, I mentioned that the Calusa and Lake People were dependent for much needed exotic materials and finished goods from outside. The environment that was their kingdom could not supply the materials required for sophisticated technological systems needed for their ritual landscapes and canals. A unique cultural variation was they ran a huge trade deficit, importing more physical goods, including all ceramics, than exporting and doing this for twenty-five centuries. The Neolithic period has this scenario play out constantly, especially with metal technology in the Bronze Age. Historically, the needy group expands and takes the needed resource or is conquered by another. There are New World variations with a different outcome, an example being the Casma/Sechin culture in Peru. Beginning in 3600 BC a group of hunter-gatherers established sacred sites in the Casma River region inland from the Pacific Coast. They practiced limited agriculture and set up their civilization and religious centers in a semiarid, desertlike environment. They built several large monumental complexes and thrived for thirty-four centuries until 200 BC, six centuries after the Glade and Calusa had built their complexes at Fort Center and Big Mound City, Florida. Around 1650 BC, another culture of hunter-gatherers one thousand miles northwest of Fort Center built a single, large ritual center in the marshlands of northeast Louisiana. They had more to trade, including much desired salt and hand-carved stone beads. But beads and salt would never offset the cost of engineering and building the Poverty Point complex.

Finally, something unique to the Calusa and Mayaimi cultures and that had to give way to totally unique cultural variations is they were the *only* culture in the Americas that lived on a peninsula with ocean on three sides. Unlike island cultures, the Calusa and Mayaimi had easy overland routes; the vast amounts of trade goods excavated at their sites, like those at Fort Center, demonstrate that dramatically. The keepers of the lake also controlled the movement of goods from east and west across the lake. But unlike the powerful, influential, and large Mississippi collections of cultures in North America, when it came to the resources of the seas, the Calusa had them in spades. Today those Florida east coast, west coast properties are some of the most desired and valued in the United States. Recently, near where I live in Port Charlotte, property sold for record $80 per square foot. It was no different in 800 BC to 1700 AD. They were and are today the highest places in a consistently low, wet, and flat/basin like environment. Then as today, coastal Florida screams culture and development. If you want to know how the Calusa and Lake People did a great deal more than subsist for twenty-five centuries, it was location, location, location. Simply put, an extreme peninsula that encompasses a well-established sacred place has to produce a culture unlike any others.

• 10 •

The Mythology and Beliefs of the Calusa and Their Neighbors

Every act of creation is first an act of destruction.

—Pablo Picasso

We believe that we invent symbols. The truth is that they invent us. We are their creatures, shaped by their hard-defining edges.

—Gene Wolfe

The Calusa and their neighbors were not easily separated from their faith, as shown by the remnants of several southern Florida tribes who were still adhering to the traditional belief system while occupying a mission at the mouth of the Miami River in 1743.

—Ryan J. Wheeler, *Treasure of the Calusa*

Other information in these accounts hints at the presence of shamanic beliefs, including curing, visions, fasting and shamanic practitioners. The Calusa and their neighbors were not easily separated from their faith.

—Ryan J. Wheeler, *Treasure of the Calusa*

If not for the abundant artifacts unearthed and cataloged during the Pepper-Hearst expedition by Frank Hamilton Cushing, all would have been lost. The Key Marco types in wood, shell, and metal have been our intimate view into the beliefs and symbols of a major contributor to prehistoric South Florida. Then again, Cushing and later Sears lucked out due to the peat and freshwater muck that protected the wood artifacts for some 950 years. Because of the seventy-by-forty-foot mortuary pond built as part of the Fort Center mortuary complex, we have a record of all those incredible carved and painted wooden animal and bird effigies found also in the prehistoric muck.

When the Calusa first migrated to the southwest Florida archipelago, they brought with them the stories, symbols, and beliefs that made them who they were. It is the beliefs revealed in symbols employed in the things made that makes one human group and their ancestors distinctive from another or in common with another. The Calusa, like so many ancient cultures, had complex symbols and beliefs. So also did the Lake People native to the lands around the great lake. One symbol could represent many things simultaneously. All myths, symbols, and beliefs had layer upon layer of meaning. Unlocking the keys to understanding these layers of meaning require skills located more on the right side of the brain. Because of this requirement, most anthropologists approach such research awkwardly and handicapped by their reliance on logic and science.

As I discussed in chapter 3, beliefs (and their symbols) are never logical, nor do they need to be. They are as a result emotionally charged. Symbols are never literal except in abstractions like letter forms and numbers. Cushing studied and practiced anthropology at a time when archaeologists searched for universally employed symbols. After returning from Key Marco, Cushing began a draft for publication of a paper that he titled "Key Marco Types." He employed the assistance of Stewart Culin to comb museum collections to gather examples of certain symbols found in the Calusa artifacts and in other Native American cultures. The curious title, I am sure, is short for "archetypes." The majority of the unfinished paper discussed a symbol that was common in the artifacts of the Calusa and many cultures, the horned bill duck (figure 10.1). This symbol Cushing believed was used by warriors on batons, shields, and canoes or worn as a protective device. Cushing's cross-cultural research of the duck symbol showed that the duck could sense danger and call the alert to quickly flee from harm. Cushing stated that he found the symbol in wood, stone, and metal. My research of the artifacts now cataloged from the Pepper-Hearst expedition indicates that they no longer exist, at least in the various housed collections at museums.

While common or more universal symbols and beliefs across Native American cultures have been researched and established by anthropologists these past 120 years, my research is primarily concerned with those that I conclude were unique to the Calusa and the Mayaimi. This includes changes in meaning to a symbol found in other societies. Jerald Milanich wrote a great deal about symbols and beliefs in *Archaeology of Precolumbian Florida*. Referencing Weeden Island culture in the sixteenth and seventeenth centuries, Milanich referenced specific beliefs and symbols he generalized as common to

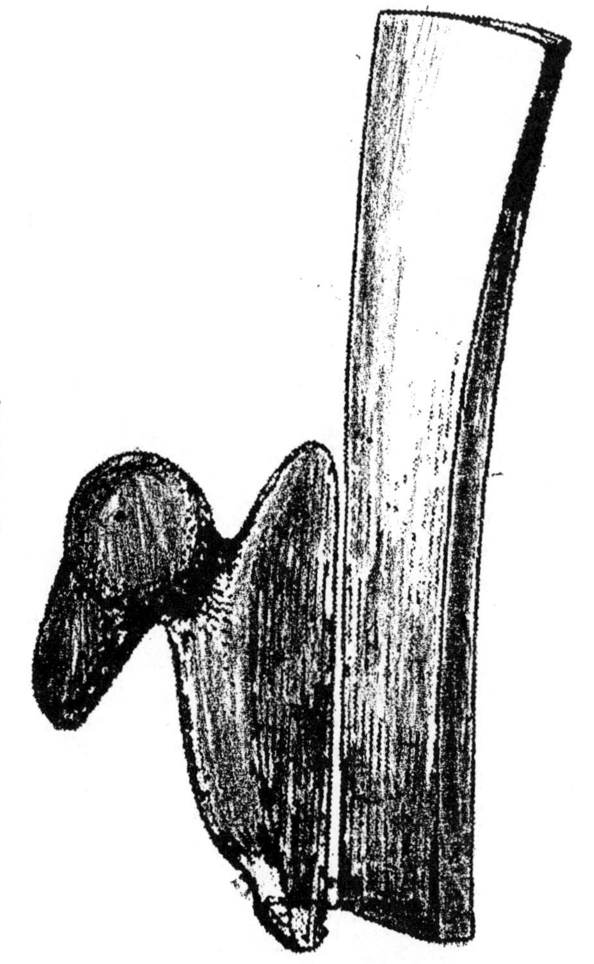

Figure 10.1. Drawing of a Calusa carved wooden horned bill duck artifact from the Key Marco site. Based on a sketch by Frank Hamilton Cushing (1896).

southeastern Native American cultures. His work has been instructive in helping me to call attention to the differences between the Calusa and Mayaimi when discussing the very same beliefs and symbols. Milanich asserted that Weeden Island people saw "humans and animals in opposition to one another." The wood carvings that characterize South Florida culture cannot be interpreted in any other way than a belief that all two-legged and four-legged birds and mammals were equal to and related to humans. Milanich asserts that water represented the underworld, a world of chaos, death, monsters, and ghosts. My research shows that water to the Calusa and Mayaimi mirrored the heavens, the opposite view of the Weeden Island people. Such a dramatic difference in symbolism indicates completely different creation stories. Finally,

Milanich stated that fire represented the sun and that the Weeden and others never extinguished ceremonial fires with water that symbolized the underworld. Cushing wrote that fire was ceremonially used in Calusa burials and was quickly put out by water, the symbol of life. In short, all of these represent major differences in beliefs.

There is a symbol found in carved wooden amulets and in alter pieces found by the Cushing Expedition at Key Marco (figure 10.2). For me, it is the unifying symbol for the entire South Florida cultural expression. Sawyer's watercolor depicts a design with a top and lower portion connected by two small squares. The design is completely symmetrical with a large, abstracted tall tree with two branches. Symbolically, the tree also mirrors a human with arms reaching up, a version of the classic peace symbol. A single leaf representing all plants is carved on both sides of the great tree. On the lower panel are three concentric circles with a center point, and a fourth and innermost circle has strong symbolic identity work and gives not only a possible insight into the creation/origin myth of the Calusa but also a version of one of the oldest creation symbols found around the world. The Tree of Life as well as the creation symbol of the Lake People are the four concentric circles. My theory about the symbols is that they had the same powerful, unifying nature as the cross in Christianity.

Another symbol found on the reverse side painted or carved are strands knotted in the middle. This symbol of unity could reference the alliance of the Calusa with their neighbors, similar to a marriage where the parties tie the knot (figure 10.3). This symbol often appears over the crescent moon symbol, a symbol for renewal and new beginnings. The research studies evince a wide variety of anthropological interpretations for the ceremonial symbol elements. In the last several decades, the altar piece or amulets have been displayed and interpreted upside down. The symbol found in numerous locations, a total of fifty-eight by 2000, was also made out of incised copper and carved stone, as well as wood. Anthropologist George Luer did a survey of the tablets in 2000 when a metal tablet was unearthed in downtown metropolitan Tampa. The most recent one was found in 2003 at a burial mound excavation, Blueberry, near Lake Istokpoga in Highlands County, 140 miles from where Cushing found the first tablet of carved wood on Marco Island in Collier County. The archaeologist assigned to researching the tablet in Highlands County made no mention to the fifty-eight previously found versions over the entire southern region. She did determine, though, that the artist was right-handed, but the big picture, the universality of the symbol in the South Florida culture region, escaped her analysis. This underscores my call for connecting the dots. The Tree of Life is a major myth or archetype found in world history. The cosmic or original tree connects both heaven and earth. It connects the upper and

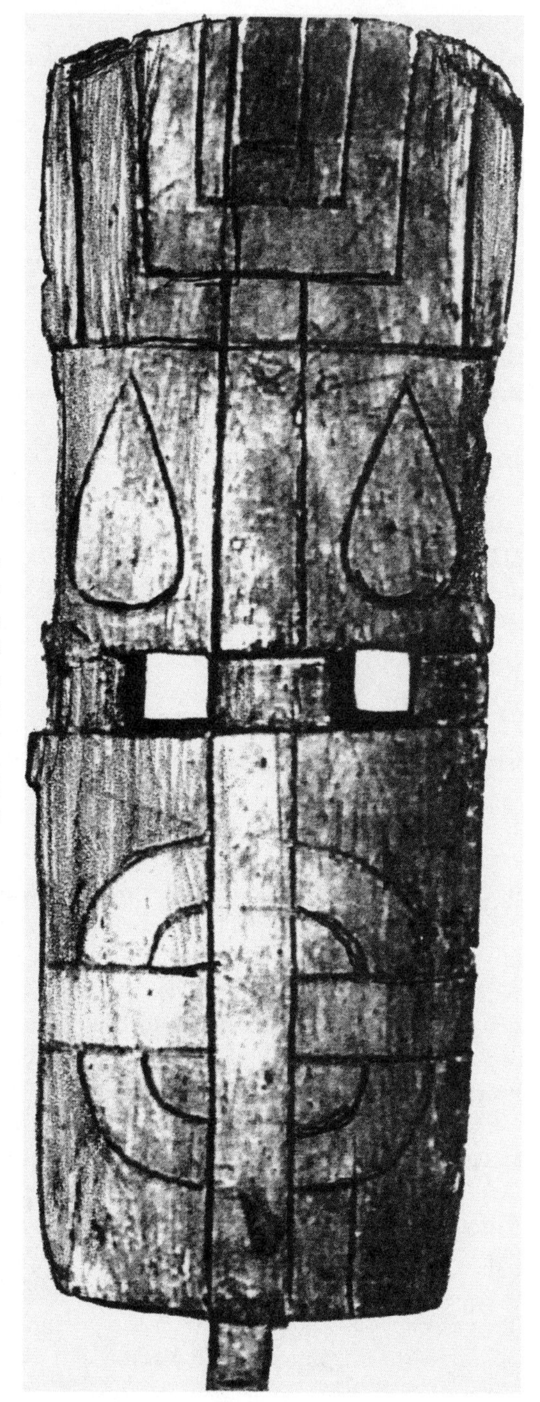

Figure 10.2. One of many Calusa carved emblems and altar pieces found throughout South Florida. The *Tree of Life* (top) is shown with two seed symbols. The universal earth symbol (bottom) has the cross that symbolized the four cardinal directions. Photo courtesy of the Special Collections Department of the University of South Florida.

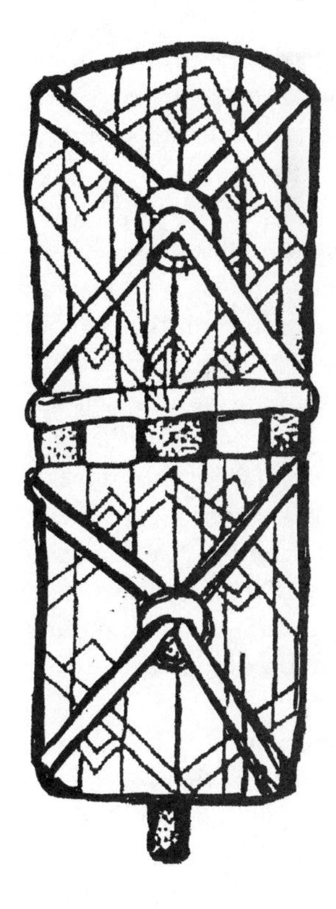

Figure 10.3. Drawing of emblem with the knotted strands motif. Drawing from artifacts found in Highlands and Pinellas counties, Florida.

lower realms. In North America it can be found in the creation myth of the Iroquois and related Eastern Woodland tribes. The creation story begins with the great tree, which is in heaven where the first humans lived until a pregnant woman fell from heaven, landing in an endless sea. The woman is saved from drowning by a giant turtle. She then formed the entire world on the back of the giant turtle by planting bark from the original tree. In this story and in all related stories, the Tree of Life brings forth all of nature—the plants, animals, and humans. This creation story with its abundance of female symbols has humans as equals with creation, all creatures, and having common ancestry with the tree. Later, the Mayans too had the symbol of the Tree of Life central to their beliefs and view of the origins of the universe. The myths differed from the Iroquois in that the Mayan tree originated in the underworld and proceeded up to connect our world and heaven. The many dark aspects of Mayan beliefs and practices logically proceed from this view.

It would then proceed that to the Calusa, trees and wood were sacred. To the Calusa, wood was not just one of any medium, it was the most important. Layer upon layer, wood was sacred, as were all the creatures the Calusa carved into the wood. This new view answers the question as to why when most tribes used clay or stone, the Calusa chose to carve wooden figures.

A predominant symbol that was incorporated into the Calusa beliefs and worldview was the conch shell. When Cushing came to the Key Marco site, there were perimeter walls of conch shells that bordered the site. Cushing repeatedly referred to the Calusa as the shell pile dwellers. Archaeologists have found data to suggest the prehistoric people on the Gulf Coast of Florida actually farmed conch for their meat and shells. Again, like the cypress, shells have had layer upon layer of meaning going back to ancient India. Many world cultures viewed the conch shell in particular as an important spiritual symbol due to its spiral shape. Together with the circle, the spiral is perhaps one of the oldest symbols used in esoteric wisdom. In Hinduism, the conch shell was important because it was associated with water and the creation of the universe. In North America, the spiral, representing the genesis of the universe and all life, can be found in cave paintings, petroglyphs, and incised pottery. Underscoring the significance of the symbol of the conch shell, Cushing and his team found conch used in the construction of Key Marco. William Sears found many conch shells used as burial goods when excavating a burial mound at Fort Center, and Luer found the king conch used to build the Acline Temple Mound in Charlotte Harbor.

Cushing in his journals made mention of a symbol found at Key Marco that he encountered in his exaction of Hopi Indian sites in the Southwest. The circle with the cross indicating the four quadrants, the four sacred directions known throughout North America and the world, appeared in Calusa amulets and carved shell gorgets (figure 6.8). This universal Neolithic symbol I discussed earlier in chapter 4. Cushing also discovered that the remains and burial goods excavated at the burial mound at Key Marco had been placed in keeping with the four quadrants. Calusa pigments used in the burials underscored the more universal use of color by tribes to reference a cardinal direction. Similarities like those symbol forms found at Key Marco fueled his later research, showing cultural similarities with a wide variety of ancient people. This cosmology was being replaced in the north by a new view and the new symbols employed by the Mississippi culture. The Calusa, unlike all other tribes east of the Mississippi, also believed in two other directions, above and below. You could say there were six cardinal directions that the Calusa employed in rites and rituals.

There is no more pervasive and important symbol found in the Calusa world than water. We all know water as the key resource for sustaining all life, but for the Calusa water was a multifaceted symbol with endless layers of meaning. To understand why the Calusa incorporated water courts and ponds with their architecture when none of their predecessors or contemporaries did would start to unravel perhaps the biggest mystery surrounding the culture.

First, one must consider the possible creation myth where the pregnant woman falls from heaven into the "endless sea." The endless sea corresponds to the "great flood" found in the majority of Neolithic creation stories. Layer upon layer, the endless sea may symbolize a memory of an actual climate event and shifting populations via migrations, the deeper symbol being the subconscious, the underworld. Economically, the more concrete symbol would be the Calusa's reliance on the sea for their food and shells. Water is one of the world's common symbols for fertility. When you consider that the Mayaimi world was constantly moving sheets of fresh water and the Calusa lived in an island kingdom surrounded by water, and it rains half of the year, that water symbolized fertility of all man, animal, and plant.

Fertility symbols abound in the artifacts from the Florida Gulf Coast. One most obvious was a phallic symbol in a metal amulet found by Wells Moses Sawyer, in which he made a drawing on page 17 of his *Florida Notebook*. The artifact went missing and cannot be found at the Smithsonian or the University of Pennsylvania. One less obvious is the "Key Marco Cat" (figure 10.4). The six-inch-tall, half-panther, half-human statuette has intrigued museumgoers for 120 years. Cats were obvious fertility symbols, and that plus the size and shape, I believe, reveal its symbolism as more than a knickknack.

Upon researching both the Calusa and Mayaimi cultures, I believe that the making of ponds and water courts were their way of making their engineered spaces mirror the sacred places. Each pond was a microcosm of the southern Florida environment. In a recent paper, Florida anthropologist Thomas Pluckhahn, revisiting Fort Center with Victor Thompson, wrote:

> Although we cannot say with certainty what kinds of rituals took place, it is likely these were communal rituals that integrated large groups of people, given the size of the Great Circle. Furthermore, given the emphasis on aquatic resources, such rituals probably referenced the contextual landscape. Particularly, we note the similarity in form of the Great Circle with other oxbow lakes in the wetland environment as well as the circular ditch that still holds water today as an interior manipulation of water. It is possible that this was to create a boundary for spirits or as reference to the continued productivity of the environment. In a similar vein, the charnel pond with its wooden platform could be a representation of the Lake Okeechobee itself, as islands in the lake were used as burial locales. Finally, the act of creation was also important in and of itself, as indicated by the burying and rebuilding of several great circles at the same locale on the landscape.

Olmec archaeologists have noted the Olmec integrated man-made ponds with their ceremonial mounds. Several have stated that to the Olmec, water symbolized fertility. There is reason to believe that to the Calusa and Mayaimi,

Figure 10.4. Key Marco cat, two views. Photograph from the Smithsonian Institution.

starting as early as 800 to 750 BC and not much later at Big Mound City, water resources were the Calusa contribution to the regional ceremonial complexes, a merging of two distinctive cultures and beliefs. Perhaps, together, they built their ponds also for use in yearly fertility rituals.

Cushing wrote in his journal that the lands from Tampa Bay to the Florida Cape is abundant with shallow lakes—chains of lakes—thousands upon thousands of ponds, and incredible spring-fed sinkholes owing to the calcareous soil that retains groundwater and the intense rainy season. Obviously, the culture would not undertake the creation of artificial ponds for decorative reasons. They served as cultural emblems unique to them and their ways. When you consider the monumental earthworks by their Mississippi culture neighbors, none of those sites had ponds or water courts. Not one.

After reading Ryan Wheeler's *Treasure of the Calusa*, I was struck by the Calusa art that depicted the red crested woodpecker (figure 10.5). I was familiar for years with the painted wood panel depicting in their naturalistic style the woodpecker, but when I saw the examples of carved woodpecker hair ornaments with metal heads, my experience told me they were a very special Calusa symbol. Wheeler also stated that examples were found all over the Mayaimi areas. I know of no other North American Woodland cultures who repeatedly used the woodpecker in their symbology. In the Southwest the flicker was common and used to symbolize the southern direction. But South Florida was the home of many birds, and big ones at that. Why would the mighty Calusa have an affinity with the woodpecker? The red crests certainly drew them to them, but I have come to believe it was the noise

Figure 10.5. Calusa woodpecker painted on wood panel from the Key Marco site. Florida Museum of Natural History.

woodpeckers made. Woodpeckers are the drumming birds. Similar but even more powerful than the spoonbill duck, woodpeckers signaled the call to war and the call to retreat.

In preparation for this book, I have tried with limited artifacts to find the Calusa and Mayaimi trickster. The trickster was one of the oldest and most universal figures in a culture's mythology. The Northwest Coastal people had the raven, the Southwest people had the coyote, but which animal was the trickster in South Florida mythology? Traits of the trickster in Indian mythology and elsewhere were disguise, fooling, and stealing. No animal in Florida has more of those qualities than the alligator. The alligator headpieces (figure 10.6) and carvings are my choice for the alligator as Calusa trickster—purely conjecture on my part, but as I have stated, the cultures had to have had a trickster in their mythology in order to have survived so many centuries.

The least mentioned symbol, one with the greatest meaning and functionality, was the feast. Anthropologists know this symbolic occasion from the study of the potlach found in the Northwest Coast cultures. As with the

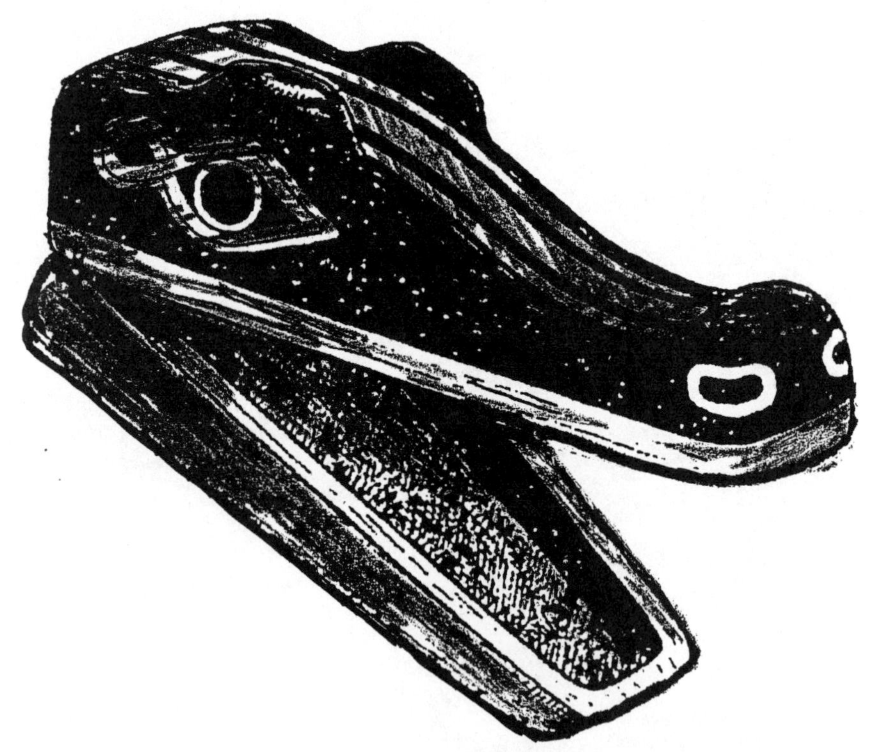

Figure 10.6. Drawing of the carved and painted Calusa alligator headpiece from the Key Marco site. Drawing based on a sketch by Frank Hamilton Cushing (1896). Ted Ehmann, 2018.

Northwest Coastal people, the feasts in South Florida were rituals that marked all changes in their society. Feasts were held for births, deaths, rites of passage, adoption, and the granting of title or office. Again, this symbol had layers upon layers of meaning. As William Sears rightfully pointed out, the Glade and for that matter the Calusa were poor in the exotic resources, resources that would have made them more technologically capable. For me, the genius of both cultures is that what they lacked in material resources, they made up for with a legacy of rituals and ceremony. Many Southeast cultures employed the same adaptive strategies such as the subcontinent of India, with its many gods and ritual celebrations, a testimony of longevity as a world culture.

Don't ask me how they knew, but the spiritual leaders of the Lake People had unparalleled wisdom. While their counterparts, the Calusa, were excessive in their outward displays, the Mayaimi were considerably more modest and simplistic. The archaeology of South Florida has proven this point for the past 120 years. What we have via the material record for the twenty-five centuries of the Lake People were the great circular ritual spaces. Simplicity in all things best characterize the Lake People, but with a simplicity proceeding from a deep metaphysical core set of beliefs. Which gods they worshipped is unknown, but what we do know is the Mayaimi religious leaders had a profound understanding of the duality of death and birth of creation and destruction. Because of Thompson and Pluckhahn's new work at Fort Center, we know that this important ceremonial center first began with the construction of the life-affirming great circle around 750 BC. Thompson and Pluckhahn state:

> The circular ditches were the part of the first events that marked increases in ritualization.

Fifty years later, next to the Great Circle, they began work on the mortuary mound. So, within a very short time, life-affirming and death-transitional ritual spaces coexisted at the Fort Center site and were the earliest manifestations of the coming together of the Mayaimi and the Calusa.

After decades of digging, no ceramics have been found in the Great Circle at Fort Center. Robert Carr has published that eight other circular ditches had been identified in South Florida. If so, it would be important to study and excavate those circles also. Looking elsewhere in global history, kivas, the circular centers found everywhere in the ruins of the Anasazi people of Four Corners in the southwestern United States, signifies a relationship as well as possible shared beliefs and cosmologies. The peaceful Anasazi from 800 AD to 1300 most likely had a dominant creation cosmology similar to the Mayaimi, using circular sacred spaces to recreate in ritual experience the oneness of all creatures and of the people.

When Thompson and Pluckhahn returned to Fort Center in 2012, they discovered that there were smaller circles within the Great Circle. They also found that circles had been destroyed and rebuilt. Such details surprisingly support a pronounced understanding of death and destruction's relationship to creation. Because I believe the Calusa and Mayaimi beliefs became shared and in common, here is what Cushing discovered. First, destruction is symbolized by puncturing a hole in the base of all ceramic burial goods. Second, after the remains and goods were placed in the mound, wood was placed over and the entire burial was set on fire. Fires in prehistoric rituals were an act of purification as well as symbolizing the needed destruction necessary for recreation. Judging from the investment in grave goods, the Calusa clearly believed the soul was reborn after death. After setting the burial on fire, Calusa spiritual leaders immediately poured water over the grave, water being the symbol of life and renewal. As opposites, the Lake People complimented the Calusa in all aspects of their material culture. You won't find the sophisticated mechanical animal headpieces, or the increased use of carved masks at lake area sites. What you do find is a culture deeply connected to the bigger picture: creation and the circle of life. Typically, such cultures were dominated by religious leaders who concerned themselves with prophecy and divination and star gazing.

• *11* •

One Land, One Culture

> The steady and at times hysterical attempts to separate the social and the biological have eroded that special position, erected a new dogma, and fragmented a promising science. Cultural anthropology with its rampant doctrine of cultural relativism, is in fact a bastard child of German romantic nationalism. As such, it is paradoxically closer to racism and fascism it fears, than is a biologically based science, whose basic tenant is Washburn's empirically established position that the human race shares 97% of their physical traits in common.
>
> —Robin Fox, *Encounter with Anthropology*

> Excellent standard archaeological work outlining the site's complicated past. I have always had the feeling however that much is lost by the process of counting and classifying pottery sherds etc. and drawing conclusions from it. Sometimes the big picture is not available throughout the minutia of this process.
>
> —Anonymous, review on Amazon.com of Thomas Pluckhahn's *Kolomoki: Settlement, Ceremony, and Status in the Deep South, A. D. 350 to 750*

After the long, dry cold spell and, before the large game disappeared from the remote lands at the tip of the Florida peninsula, the waters flowed and collected into a great lake. To the natives of the region and to the visitors, they must have felt a great sense of awe standing on the shore and not being able to see the other side of the expansive waters. If your village was there, it was time to move. The same went for the people whose villages lined the coasts. But then again, most groups moved around and very few settled. The new world that emerged during the Neolithic was dramatically different, and humans played a much bigger role in that new world. Where you could witness the dramatic change was in how humans altered the landscape.

Humans prior to the new age altered their environment for shelter or defense. But now, it was their beliefs that were changing the physical landscape, and their collective and shared beliefs. Where these believers built and invested their resources and time (usually centuries) indicated, unlike the present day, that they were chosen for what they were and not what they would become.

My research, which has used more humanized models that in total have not yet been employed in the study of prehistoric hunter-gatherer cultures, or agriculturalists in North America, has resulted in a new hypothesis as well. Even my inclusion of Milner's violence and warfare data was an effort on my part to humanize the research, such ritual violence being a common human behavior. Years after Gordon Willey's initial conclusions, only Wheeler, after viewing the data, has determined that a single culture area resulted in South Florida after twenty-five centuries. Wheeler used the concept of cultures "merging." I believe, however, that my use of global comparisons provides a more accurate account of the forces at play. My inclusion of comparisons and sequencing South Florida with Poverty Point and the hunter-gathering cultures in Louisiana, as well as returning to Willey's understanding of a larger and longer Glades epoch, provide for accessing and understanding the Calusa and Mayaimi role in a larger cultural epoch in North America. The inconvenient truth has remained—a regional culture can be determined by religion and shared beliefs and not things.

There has been a great deal of creditable research that has examined regional similarities and variations in fishing-hunter-gatherer cultures in the Southeast. That is good news. As I pointed out in chapter 2, the overspecialization in anthropology and reliance on ceramic artifacts during the latter half of the twentieth century has resulted in some pretty awful work. Among the worst of these were the studies limited to environmental models. A hallmark cultural anthropology when it began in the late 1800s was the concept of a cultural region. In Florida, there still is no agreement about cultural regions owing to rigid theories held by specialists in one culture area. Then again, more expansive thinkers, like Wheeler, get trapped in unsupportable taxonomies of Goggin, Sears, and Milanich. Julian Granberry's recently published book takes what linguistic data is available and reveals a more complete picture of the cultures in South Florida. Like me, Granberry criticizes past research by specialists that has resulted in a less-than-comprehensive view of the Calusa. Linguistics has been a missing piece, and we should all be grateful for the contribution. Granberry draws attention to the previous dependence by researchers on ceramic artifacts for constructing a view of a culture.

> This non-necessary linkage of language and artifactual data—so evident in the world—round through all time periods—has simply been ignored by present-day Florida archaeologists, who on the contrary by and large see a necessary connection between language and artifact.

To rely solely on ceramics as the ultimate determinant of culture areas and boundaries, as many have, I believe has not produced accurate accounts. As far as my area, South Florida, ceramics has been the last place to look for defining an authentic culture region. However, Willey's conclusions that there was a predominant South Florida culture early around the Tampa Bay region and lasting until 1700 could only be possible because of the repeated abundance of Glades ceramics at sites that far north of the South Florida culture region.

The dictionary defines the concept of a cultural region in anthropology as referring to "a geographical area with one relatively homogeneous human activity or complex of activities (culture)." Cultural spheres of influence may also overlap or form concentric structures of macro cultures encompassing smaller local cultures, as Wheeler professes. Different boundaries may also be drawn depending on the particular aspect of interest such as religion. My hypothesis is that South Florida was a distinct cultural region, distinctive from all cultural regions to the north. The Calusa and the Mayaimi were homogeneous in their fishing activity and most important in the complex of activities, beliefs, and ritual activities and complexes that resulted from cultural synthesis. The smaller cultures, the Tequesta and others, were drawn in via the regional ritual expression. Granberry's research and the linguistic accounts by Escalante Fontaneda, who lived with the Calusa, shows that all of the people of South Florida spoke the same language. Granberry has even traced all the tribes in South Florida back to their origins in northeast Louisiana in the Archaic period. I theorize that rather than being subjugated by the Calusa, the Mayaimi and others worked in a cooperative relationship. Paying tribute was much different than being subjected or dominated, one being forced and the other being a display of respect. Shared language, culture, and purpose therefore accounts for the cultural region lasting for twenty-five centuries. Unlike Wheeler, Milanich, and Goggin, I believe the Calusa were the catalyst for a cultural flourishing and synthesis unlike any in the prehistory of North America.

Basically, my hypothesis works well in reverse. We know that by the sixteenth century the Calusa held great sway and influence all throughout South Florida. So how did they get to that point? Thus far, the only anthropologists I feel are the most capable of understanding just what transpired in prehistoric South Florida are from outside the archaeology of Florida and South Florida. They are anthropologists whose conclusions not only fully understand the findings, but also their conclusions are supported by common sense. I am referring to anthropologists like Jon L. Gibson and John E. Clark and their body of research on Southeastern mound-building societies and hunter-gatherers. Separately they have tackled, what I believe, is the most important question about these early mound-building hunter-gatherers. That being said, why would hunter-gatherers agree to devote so much time and effort to construct such monumental earthworks? In a particularly lucid argument, Gibson remarked:

> Power, raw power, wonder-working power, is often delivered through the word and the messenger, particularly when people already agree with the message. And if first mounds and mound building were nothing else, they represented new ideas—maybe not radically different visions but certainly new ways of upholding old ideas.

Something at play in South Florida and world history repeatedly throughout the Neolithic period supports my hypothesis that the Calusa ways and beliefs, when introduced into the Glades area or vice versa, sparked the construction of regional canal systems and served large and dedicated ritual complexes. I agree with Gibson, that it was the power of ideas and not the political power at play in both Poverty Point and later in the Lake Okeechobee region.

In preparation for this book, I spoke with many Calusa researchers. Every one of them espoused the dogma preached by the University of Florida Department of Anthropology for the past forty years. Led by Dr. Marquardt, the leading Calusa specialist, that view was that the environment determined what the Calusa did and as a result who they were. As you have read in chapter 4, my research and theories based on the same data paints an entirely different picture. It was the beliefs that determined what the Calusa and others did in response to the environment. It was the beliefs that determined who they were. Over the past few decades, Marquardt and those connected with the Randell Research Center division of the University of Florida have spent their time and money researching and proving environmental change benchmarks, such as lower sea levels accounted for cultural changes. I have repeatedly tried to show them that any such environmental changes could produce a wide variety of responses based on the beliefs of the particular culture. World history proves this fact repeatedly that if *a* happens the response for all cultures is not necessarily *b* but rather *b to z*.

Contemporaries such as Thompson, Pluckhahn, Lawres, and Colvin have successfully shifted the research away from Fort Center as an agriculturalist village. Together they are theorizing about the several related ritual complexes by hardened and distinctly hunter-gatherers. Why they will not venture into

Figure 11.1. Florida and Caribbean Islands from space. Lake Okeechobee is clearly visible from the NASA satellite. Tsado/Alamy stock photo.

causation theories for the apparent cultural phenomena, I cannot reason. Especially since other contemporaries have put forth theories that would assist them. One such is John E. Clark:

> I think the evidence is clear that these sites were planned as totalities at high levels of precision and constructed over relatively short periods of time. All indicators are that these enclosed spaces served as sacred places. The conjecture is hardly earth-shaking as these sites are presumed to have been special.

To this, my theory extends the consideration of built sacred places to a particular global phenomena with roots in human's earliest religious beliefs and practices, the designation of certain natural features as sacred places. Only the most biased and or blind of anthropologists would ignore this history, given it is still playing out all over the world today.

Any worthy theory about the settled people and cultures of South Florida from 800 BC to 1700 AD must not only weigh the totality of evidence of commonality in their way of life, the shared environment, and decisions against horticulture, but also the probability of shared beliefs. I completely understand the reluctance of working anthropologists to venture into theories that deal with the beliefs and rituals of hunter-gatherer cultures. After 120 years of anthropology, it is still virgin territory. The conundrum, however, is that if you chose to explain a phenomenon such as hunter-gatherers in South Florida with no exotic resources who built and rebuilt not one but four immense mound complexes seemingly dedicated to religious rituals, you will have to include the beliefs that empowered such activity. Faulty theories on the topic are those of the University of California, Berkeley, anthropologists Frank Marlowe and Harvey Peoples, who theorized that emerging leaders "used the concept of a supernatural moral enforcer to manipulate others into cooperation" and thus dismissed the history of the transition from sacred sites to urban centers. Marlowe, who did fieldwork in Tanzania with one of the last remaining groups of hunter-gatherers, sadly generalized that all "simple egalitarian hunter-gatherer groups generally hold fewer religious beliefs and participated in less ritual." Like Sears, who could not believe that hunter-gatherers could not have built Fort Center, Marlowe believes that hunter-gatherers are incapable of complex beliefs and rituals. While difficult to argue with few studies to support your theory, there is always the freedom of having a blank tablet and simply trusting in your observations.

There will be many who will argue that my returning to the original view of South Florida prehistory as a "single cultural region" is a big step backward. When Milanich in 1994 determined, based on research starting in 1948, that South Florida was three cultural regions, he assumed that progress had been made. After all, he has continually called attention to the northern regions of Florida having the majority of research. This trend continues twenty-five years later—plain ceramics, little interest. As discussed in chapter 3, Milanich, based on very few researched sites and the premature taxonomies of Goggin and Sears, stated there were actually three regions: Okeechobee, Caloosahatchee, and Glades. At the conclusion of his subchapter on the Caloosahatchee region in *Archaeology of Precolumbian Florida*, he articulated what would be a worthy question for any or all anthropological research in South Florida:

> It is likely that cultural and perhaps political relationships between the two regions were closer than suggested by our present taxonomy which divides them into separate areas. As yet this aspect of south Florida cultural dynamics has not been adequately explored. Indeed our present taxonomy focusing on the uniqueness of each of these regions may be hindering archaeological studies to articulate relationships between them.

By delegating a cultural region to a subregion would mean these cultures would have been impossible to defend. There is no way each of them could have survived given the immense size and power of the northern neighbors, the Weeden Island chiefdoms. Warfare was a reality and safety was in numbers. The South also lacked all of the critical hard minerals that collectively all groups in the region needed to negotiate through trade in order to possess any or all of those vital natural resources. You could never say that about the culture areas in the northern parts of Florida during those periods.

There is credible evidence that Willey's and Goggin's view of a "single culture area" were correct, but not for the reasons they stated. I have attempted to show that there were very similar cultural traits for the fishing-hunter-gatherer groups in the Southeastern portion of North America during the late Archaic period. Of course, the most obvious were they were egalitarian societies and as such not complex or socially stratified in any way. There was one variant, that being around 1800 to 1650 BC, several groups merged, had a unifying set of beliefs, and built the Archaic period monumental earthworks at Poverty Point. Leading archaeologist on the subject and quoted in this book believe that the labor and resources used to build Poverty Point were volunteered. I have provided the world history comparisons, because what they did was a first. Such monumental works in the Old World were constructed by extremely stratified and agriculturally based societies. Even the beliefs and religion were imposed on the people by the ruling elite. As Poverty Point was abandoned, probably due to a period of continuous warfare, the Calusa arrived from that area and settled in the southern Gulf coastal archipelago. There they encountered a diverse group of small societies who were native to the area. Willey's work in 1949 gives us a complete picture of a vast southern culture region with shared beliefs, ceramics, tools, and by 800 BC, shared mortuary and burial practices. Perhaps the most important to the newly arrived Calusa around 500 BC were the Mayaimi, the Lake People. Not only were the Mayaimi the people of the sacred lake and known for their beliefs and rituals, they also controlled the critical trade route from the west to the east coast. There is much evidence, if you remove the bias and predispositions I mentioned in chapter 1, as well as avoid the disagreements and disregard of narrow-minded professionals, to support a progression from many to one in South Florida. After all, South Florida by the seventeenth century was the only region that had not adopted agriculture. By comparison, all the other culture regions were marked by a series of short-lived and competing cultures. Escalante Fontaneda's memoirs show that the Calusa culture region actually increased measurably and expanded further north by 1500. The Calusa and Mayaimi also left behind a tangible group of symbols in wood, stone, and metal depicting the tree of life, the world cosmos, and the knotted strands of their cherished regional unity and set of beliefs. How else can you interpret those symbols and their frequency?

I am content to work on a train of thought introduced by Jon L. Gibson, that being "new ideas" that came into South Florida by 500 BC. That I attribute the new ideas to the arrival of the Calusa is more than plausible. That it was not only sufficient but also powerful enough to sustain cultural and political order and continuity for the remaining 2,200 years is a very plausible theory. Gibson, who has researched the Poverty Point site in a remote area of northern Louisiana, involves exactly some of the same questions since the monumental earthworks by hunter-gatherers who predate southern Florida's by eight hundred years. So, the lake region of South Florida is not without prehistoric precedent, with the exception of the total number and scale of the sites and systems of canals that facilitated movement of goods, communication, and transportation to ritual centers providing for a total unification of the region. Nathan Lawres and Matthew Colvin, both graduate students, are currently the only researchers looking at the relationships between the multiple sites. More researchers and more research will be critical. Perhaps it will take a process like that at Poverty Point, where more and more people walked the site and were overwhelmed by the magnitude of the effort. Witnesses who have recently visited Big Mound City in the J. W. Corbett Wildlife Management Area have remarked about how long it took to take it all in. When dealing with prehistoric ceremonial earthworks measured in football fields, that might provide the long-needed impetus to explore.

Beginning in 1948, prominent and emerging archaeologists stopped researching and investigating the Calusa. They did this not because there was nothing new to discover. Quite the contrary: very little was yet known, and who the Calusa were and their origins was still a puzzle. The fact remains that what brought Florida archaeology and prehistory to national focus was the discovery of the Calusa artifacts in the late 1900s. John Goggin found a plain, sand-tempered, and very utilitarian style of ceramics throughout the entire southern portion of Florida, including those occupied and controlled by the Calusa. He alone designated the majority of the South Florida culture region as the Glades region, supplanting the Calusa. But in 1948, the focus of archaeology turned to a complex of ceremonial mounds near Lake Okeechobee called Fort Center. Despite the presence of major Calusa materiality at Fort Center and only the plain ceramics not unique to just the lake area to describe the occupants, William Sears in 1982 concluded that a previously unknown and unrecognized culture was responsible for the ceremonial complex, stating that he discovered proof of maize cultivating at Fort Center. Without further study and research, the Calusa went out of fashion as a worthy culture to research.

It is my opinion as a layperson that in the postwar period in Florida, the archaeology got ahead of the anthropology. I am mindful that ceramics are datable indicators of a culture, their chronology, and geographic borders. Ceramics are not, however, the end all and be all. In South Florida prehistory, ceramics played a very insignificant role. The plain ceramics are most likely a cultural diffusion from Georgia 2,500 years prior, and it shows little change over twenty-five consecutive centuries. It never improved, indicating its importance to the cultures living in South Florida. In short, it was secular and strictly common and utilitarian. That archaeologists beginning in 1948 would base the entire taxonomy and thus the prehistoric narrative for twenty-five centuries on Glades ware seems a bridge too far and simply an attempt to connect North and South Florida and explain away the possibility of a distinctly southern culture.

In 2010, William F. Keegan wrote a paper about the use of ceramics for defining cultures in the Caribbean region and illustrating how as a model it has not provided reliable results. Returning to the author of the "cultural-historical model," Florida's Irving Rouse, he describes how Rouse developed the model while excavating in the 1930s. Goggin and then Sears learned and employed that model. Keegan wrote that Rouse:

> recognized the need (also) to consider language, biology, material culture, and ethnohistory (which includes religion and beliefs) in order to adequately describe a prehistoric culture.

Because there were few to no researchers in the other areas, ceramics would have to do the work of all of them. Researchers have always had Moore's ethnographies. They finally have the linguistics piece from Granberry, tracing of the Calusa language to the Tunica of northeast and Gulf Coast Louisiana. Because of Granberry's work, there now is linguistic evidence to support new research connecting the monumental earthworks at Poverty Point with those a little later at Fort Center in South Florida. We have linguistic evidence for both Louisiana and Florida anthropologists of a diaspora because of a yet-to-be-determined event or events, leading to a great migration out of the area and into South Florida. So, rather than being foreclosed on the Calusa, foreclosed on the involvement of the Calusa in the lake area complexes, there is a whole new area for significant anthropological contributions.

The subject of diasporas has intrigued me since the weekend I spent in the late 1990s with a Mayan priest, the elder who was in the area at the invitation of both the University of Pennsylvania and atomic physicists at Princeton. He carefully explained to a small group how the Mayan people did not die off, but rather that they dispersed. What they took with them were profound understandings of life, the universe, and things to come. If you have ever witnessed the Hopi elders, you will understand the esoteric wisdom of many aboriginal cultures, a wisdom I have gleaned from the lake people in South Florida and the many great circular ritual centers they began to build in 800 BC.

Developing a reliable ethnography for South Florida prehistory is long overdue. I wish to encourage anthropologists to take the lead. Much can be accomplished by reviewing previous work, as I have done here. After all, as Willey reported in the mid-twentieth century, the sites are now gone. As I hope I have successfully illustrated, it is not the shortcomings of the subject, but rather the shortcomings of the observers.

• 12 •

Visiting the Calusa and Mayaimi Sites

Where must we start in trying to re-understand ourselves? . . . We must condemn as deficient any commentary on the human condition that fails to take into account the ancientness of the species and the more than five-million years of natural selection that has molded the questionable end product that includes the commentators and their commentaries.

—Robin Fox, *Encounter with Anthropology*

At the middle of the twentieth century a very great part, I should say well over half, of the archaeological sites of all types on the Gulf Coast of Florida have been seriously damaged or completely destroyed.

—Gordon Willey, *Archaeology of the Florida Gulf Coast*

The process of researching the prehistoric people of South Florida has made me keenly aware of major shortcomings in how the State of Florida, its residents and officials have dealt with the wealth of prehistoric archaeological sites. Gordon Willey's assessment of the damage to and the destruction of sites on the Gulf Coast by 1949 fell on deaf ears. In the southern portion of the state, archaeological sites of the significance of those in the Kissimmee Valley, Lake Okeechobee, and Everglades culture region belong to all the people and future generations of the world. Educating each generation about world history and of their importance in protecting and preserving this heritage is a collective responsibility. I am a retired teacher and refuse to accept a world where children can not have access to real history. Even though the majority of the sites were destroyed does not mean their records and data should likewise be lost. The average student is not going to do the research in the literature to find out about the many prehistoric sites in their neighborhoods researched by anthropologists and their knowledge kept from public view. Preservation inherently creates conflict by removing most human activity and exploits resource in designated parcels. Protection, the function of government, often involves a restriction of public access to places that are environmentally sensitive or that incorporate archaeological sites. Florida, like most states, has comprehensive and strict laws to protect archaeological sites (figure 12.1). But like most states, it lacks policies and funding to prioritize, effectively protect, and develop certain sites for public access. The Florida Division of Historical Resources was established within the state department with the preservation of historic and archaeological sites. This mission was to include the work necessary to have sites designated as National Historic Places, as well as National Historic Landmarks. For over a year now, I have taken on the research and proposal to have the Fort Center site nominated as a National Historic Landmark. While the staff has offered feedback, they are helpless in that they have no budget, including travel expenses necessary for such an effort. Because of the department's shortcomings, it falls on individuals to spend their time and money. The staff repeatedly instructed me to enlist professional archaeologists in the project. Each professional I tried to enlist to help, including those who worked at the Fort Center site and published their findings, declined the invitation. Recently, I attempted to get assistance and a permit to take a group to the site, and the Department of Fish and Wildlife, who manage the land where the site sits, would not assist us. While anyone can park and walk the

Figure 12.1. No trespassing sign near mounds.

one-and-a-half miles to the site (three miles total for the trip), people my age simply cannot make the trip without the gate being unlocked and the ability to drive directly to the site on a road designed for that purpose.

Local, county, and state governments have always had the power to purchase property for preservation. The Portavant Temple Mound within the Emerson Point Preserve in Palmetto, Manatee County, is a good example of accessibility to an important prehistoric cultural resource. Many early archaeological sites were made into public parks and museums. Then there are always large tracts of land that are already public. Florida, like many states, has a department just for archaeology on public land. Currently Florida ranks fourteenth in the percentage of state or federal lands, a total of 26.4 percent of all state acreage. A large portion of that, however, is federally owned and managed areas in the Everglades. Florida has a wealth of state parks, which along with many wildlife areas make up the 26.4 percent of public lands.

Figure 12.2. Map of four archaeological state parks in Florida. Ted Ehmann.

There are 112 state parks, four of which are also archaeological state parks or .00357 percent of the state parks (figure 12.2). Of importance to my research and my advocating for the preservation and the accessibility of South Florida mounds, Florida's creation of state parks, especially in the interior region, has been disproportionate (figure 12.3).

In 1966, Congress passed the National Heritage Preservation Act. Prehistoric and Native American heritage sites could be protected when qualified and registered as National Historic Landmarks. There are currently forty-eight designated National Historic Landmarks in Florida. Soon after, the United Nations followed suit and created UNESCO, a registry of world cultural and natural heritage sites. There are approximately twenty-five world sites in the United States. In Florida, Everglades National Park is a UNESCO site (figure 12.4). It is also the only UNESCO site in North America on the UN "In Danger" List. In 2003 President Bush signed executive order 13287 moving on continued preservation with an emphasis on education. The term *heritage tourism* was adopted, and some states attempted to develop heritage tourism departments. When a state, county, or local government takes an important archaeological site, develops the site, and manages it as a state park, the following happens. First the site becomes fully accessible to the public. Accessibility legally includes people with disabilities. Second, the site produces revenue from tourism. Third, heritage tourism creates well-needed jobs and helps support secondary jobs and economies. Archaeological sites as state, county, or municipal parks or national parks, and archaeological sites as UNESCO World Heritage Sites, do all of the above while protecting the site for future generations.

Currently, in the South Florida prehistoric culture region that is the focus of this book, there are presently over 1,450 recorded prehistoric archaeological sites according to the state master file data. Of those the majority have not been excavated or assessed. More than likely they have been destroyed by development. The state and counties and organizations like the Florida Public Archaeological Network rely on volunteers and cannot possibly handle the overwhelming job of monitoring sites and protecting them from destruction by natural and human causes. The record shows that even when the state and archaeologists are directly involved with an important archaeological site, proper preservation measures are not taken. In South Florida, two tragic examples bear this out. In the 1960s, the State of Florida approved William Sears's excavation of the Fort Center site in Glades County. He left the site in bad shape. Even after he published his book on the importance of the Fort Center site, he failed to protect it, and he never completed the paperwork to have the site added to the National Registry of Historic sites. Thirty-six years later, Florida has yet to have Fort Center designated even as a National His-

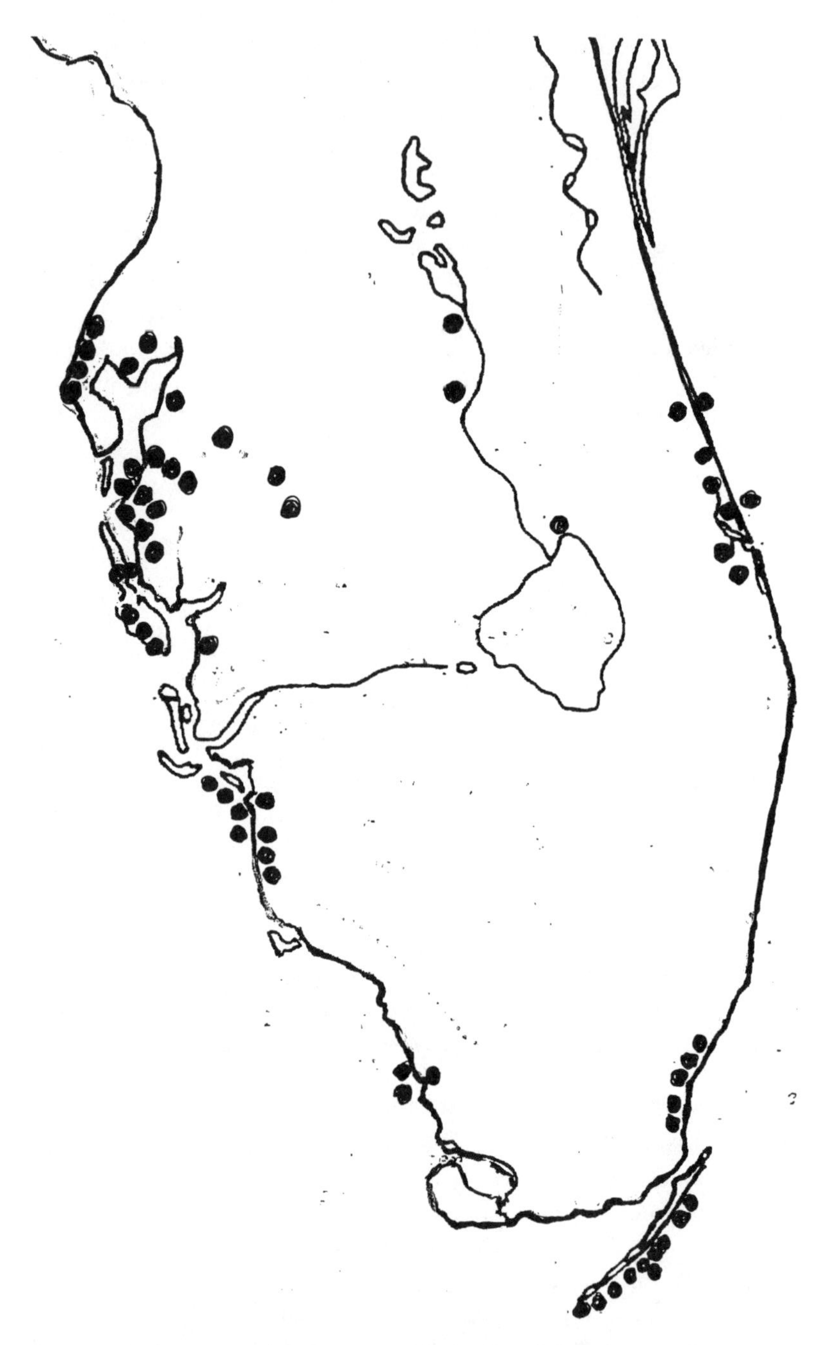

Figure 12.3. Map showing the state parks in Florida and the conspicuous lack of state parks in the cultural resource-rich area of South Central Florida. Ted Ehmann.

toric Place. Fort Center, which houses the feature that is at the forefront of this book and its title, the Great Circle, was owned by the Lykes Brothers, one of Florida's leading cattle concerns. They still maintain grazing rights to the new corridor. After a long legal battle with the state, the Lykes Brothers sold rights to the state, and the state's Fish and Wildlife Department became the managers. A commission was set up, and recreationists and environmentalists decided the fate of one of the most significant archaeological sites by hunter-gatherers in world history. The agreement served the needs of hunters, hikers, and canoers, but excluded the need for accessibility by those in the public concerned with the archaeology. They banned all vehicles. The closing of the road for that use resulted in forcing anyone who wants to visit the site to walk in the sun for three hours. My first visit nearly killed me.

Again, in the early 1980s archaeologist Michael Russo was called in to see if there were any archaeological sites on Horr's Island next to Marco Island. Developers were planning an exclusive gated community with million-dollar vacation homes called, ironically, Key Marco. Russo and his team discovered the oldest burial mound in North America, other important mounds, and a ritual shell ring dating to 3500 BC. He never argued that the site was significant and did the paperwork to have it registered as a National Historic Site. He submitted his work for a doctoral dissertation, got his PhD, and is now in charge of designating National Historic Sites. The significant sites on Horr's Island sit on people's lawns. The exclusive community built on the ancient site is gated; therefore, if you wish to visit, you are trespassing.

Of the thirty-six prehistoric sites in the South Florida cultural region that are known and that I have reviewed, only nine are accessible to the public (figure 12.4). Sites like Mound Key can be difficult and demanding. Not only are the others not accessible to visit, but even their locations are not accessible and kept secret. There are two Calusa sites you can visit in Lee County. Both are on the National Register. First there is the Randell Research Center in Pineland, Pine Island, Florida, registered as the Pineland District. There is parking, facilities, guided tours, and an admission. The Randell Research Center is part of the Battey's Landing Calusa mound complex with canals, first researched in 1896 by Frank Hamilton Cushing (figure 9.4). The second was the capitol of the Calusa chiefdom, Mound Key State Park. Mound Key State Archaeological Park is in Estero Bay and is only available by boat. There are no facilities. It is definitely too difficult for young children, seniors, and people with disabilities. There is the Miami Circle in Miami Dade County, which was a Tequesta ceremonial site. However, the city covered the interesting prehistoric limestone circle with sod, leaving only the perimeter markers and a small historic marker. Had they left the circle, built a replica of the Indian round building, and created an information center, it would be well worth a visit.

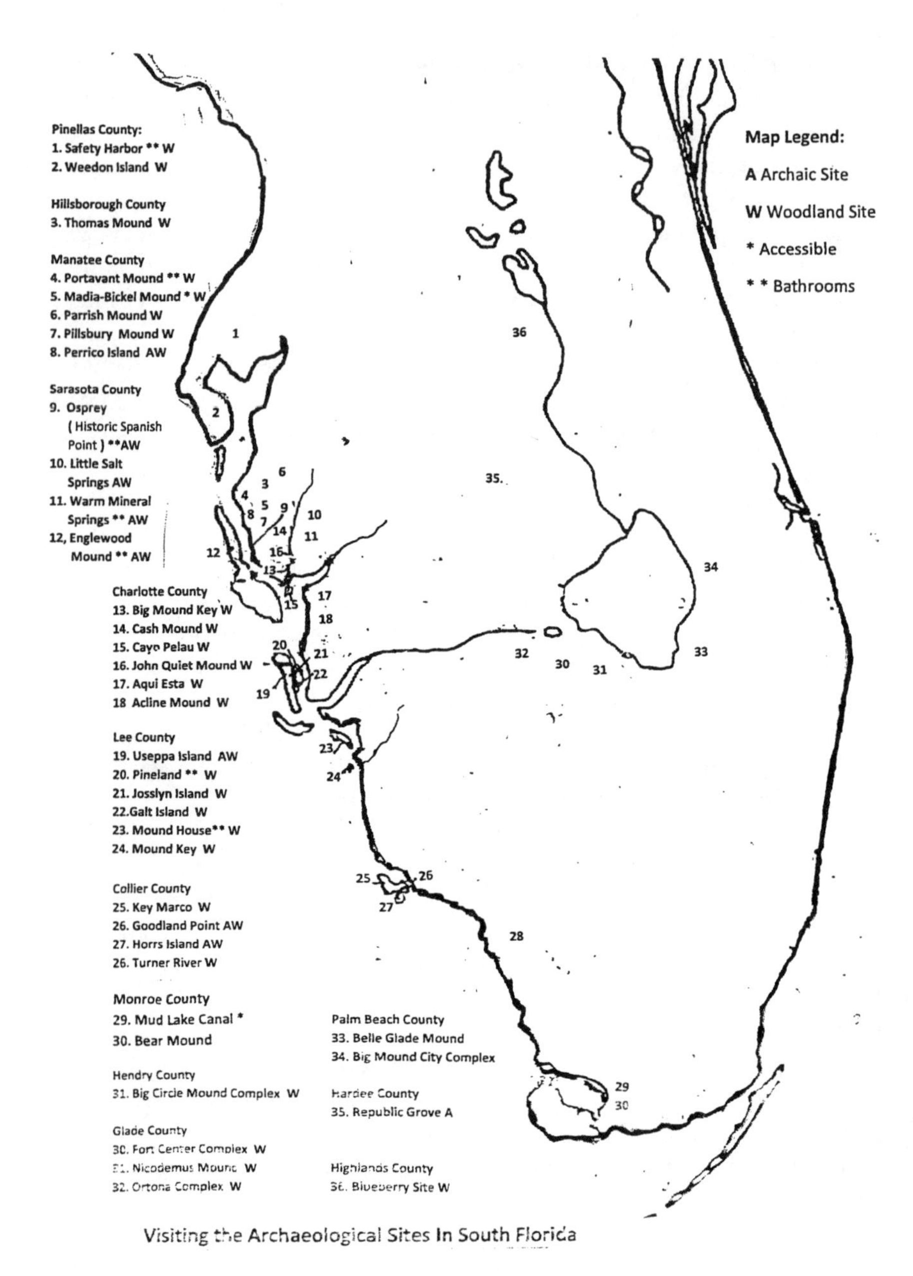

Figure 12.4. Map of mound sites in South Florida showing which ones are accessible to the public. Ted Ehmann.

Two other archaeological sites in remote southern locations in the culture region are in Monroe County. Bear Lake Mounds has a trail, but once there the boardwalk and the site suffered damage from Hurricane Wilma and was closed as of 2005. Around the bend is another site registered as a National Historic site, Mud Lake Canals. This site demonstrates the size of the Calusa influence, in which they engineered a system of vital connecting canals as far south as Cape Sable. There is no visitor center or facilities, and like Fort Center, you are on your own.

Close to home and to my heart where I live in Charlotte County is the Big Mound Key Site (figure 9.4B). The Calusa built a mound and ridge complex, which mirrors the Poverty Point site in Louisiana with its series of semicircular ridges (see figure P.2). The remote site within the Charlotte Harbor State Preserve is unmatched. Very little research has been done on the unusual site, and none has been published. The remote site, unsecured for centuries, was vandalized in 1982 by treasure hunters. Despite public outcry, when the news was reported, Charlotte County did not respond to the need to protect and preserve the site. Charlotte County is unique in that they have no historical and prehistorical preservation policy. For decades, the officials are all too willing to let the sites go by the wayside. They later installed a historic marker that references the once important structure. In 2020, the county will celebrate its centennial. Unlike its neighboring counties, Charlotte County will have very little of its history to show. As recently as Charlotte County's April 26, 2007, planning document, dozens of prehistoric cultural resources were included for protection. Now the Charlotte County 2050 plan retains the Big Mound Key site (figure 9.4B) and abandons all of the others.

Returning to the subject of heritage tourism, heritage tourists actively seek out places to visit and vacation that are "authentic." They seek towns and cities, therefore, that have areas and structures of historic value. It is not a difficult prospect to understand. Preserving and maintaining local historic structures is rewarded by a significant increase in tourism, while building local pride in the history of a community. I was bewildered when Charlotte County rejected out of hand my proposal in 2018 to include heritage tourism in all their future tourism development plans. The Calusa had Charlotte Harbor as their heartland for twenty-five centuries, but under generations of county government, this has not even earned their legacy and street names or buildings that bear their name.

When I moved to Charlotte County in 2016, I accessed online the Florida Department of Tourism website for a heritage tour of southwestern Florida archaeological sites. To my surprise and disappointment, my area was in the middle of an archaeological dead zone. The state's tour ended one day in Sarasota County with a visit to Historic Spanish Point in Osprey. The location houses the Palmer archaeological site. Then there are seventy-two miles of nothing until the tour takes you to Pineland, in Lee County, where you visit the Randell Research Center's Calusa canal, pond, and mounds. An added reason to undertake the writing of this book was the need to communicate to the public that for centuries, Charlotte Harbor was the heartland of a prehistoric culture with earthworks throughout the entire region. It was and is the very opposite of a dead zone, and this reality is well known by the officials entrusted with the historical resources.

Florida, when it comes to the listing, preservation, and public accessibility to prehistoric heritage sites, is consistent with the other states of the union. It is not because in the United States we as a people don't value them, it is because we were never taught their importance. Values are taught in our schools through the process of enculturation. The American culture through the primary and secondary education curriculum are taught what to value. History is taught, and most students hate it. Prehistory is not. This is why I went to great time and expense to create a prehistory unit to begin the study of world history. I was a student who loved history, but even as a child, common sense told me that human prehistory, which is 2.5 million years old, had a great more to teach us about humans than the more recent five thousand years. Therefore, when you view a map of Nationally Registered Historic Places in Florida, a state with a rich prehistory and most of the structures are historic, that is the reason. Everyone has been taught to value and be interested in history.

In previous chapters I discussed the problem of continuing narratives about prehistory that have been proven to be incorrect. I also mentioned just how difficult it has been to have new archaeological discoveries included in the prehistoric narrative. Anthropologists and archaeologists are to blame for this state of affairs. Generations of Americans still believe that the first Indians migrated to North and South America via the Bering Strait. Recent archaeological research has humans living in Brazil around thirty thousand years ago. In Florida, most students don't know that recently the remains of a Paleolithic individual named Vero Man was discovered near Vero Beach and dates back to fourteen thousand years ago. I would be remiss not to talk about the fifteen known Archaic period sites found throughout the state, five of which are in the cultural region of South Florida. Windover Pond Site in Brevard County is the site of prehistoric bog burials, and the site is registered and accessible. Warm Mineral Springs is registered and accessible for bathing with a fee. Nearby Little Salt Springs, registered, also in Sarasota County, was accessible but is now closed to the public. This treatment of Archaic period sites and those even earlier in Florida is foolish considering most states have no such prehistoric sites. As far as I am concerned they are wasted public treasures.

On one of the wilderness trails in South Florida, I happened upon a sign put there by the state. The sign alerted hikers to the fact that the original people considered the area sacred and asked people hiking in the area to respect the environment. Returning to what values we as a culture impart to our young, this sign draws attention to the significance of the Calusa and Glades people. By protecting, preserving, and developing the more important archaeological sites in South Florida for tourism, the important and relevant lessons of Florida's original people will be available for all future generations. National parks, national monuments, and world heritage sites are responsible for tens of billions of dollars in revenue each year. They provide for thousands of jobs and support thousands of secondary jobs related to services. A report on the growing trend in ecotourism, a similar demographic to historic tourism, resulted in $60 billion in revenue in 2014, with only a cost amount of $10 billion. Looking at a map showing state parks, the entire South Florida archaeological culture region is empty. The area is one of the most sparsely populated, undeveloped, and poor areas of Florida. If ever there was a win/win opportunity for heritage tourism and a region, the areas surrounding the great lake is it. After all, if my theories are correct, then such development of these important monumental ritual sites into accessible, teachable, and living monuments would continue a tradition started by the Calusa and Mayaimi people 2,900 years ago: that being thousands of people traveling great distances to a sacred place to experience a oneness, a connection, and a relatedness to the world and all that dwells within and without.

• *13* •

Time, Money, and the Public

Lack of direction, not lack of time, is the problem. We all have twenty-four-hour days.

—Zig Ziglar

To sum up my advice to young people who want to study archaeology is this. Become an engineer, a doctor or a lawyer, work four days a week at this well paid and fulfilling job, devote the fifth day to amateur archaeology.

—Balm

Since retiring to Florida, I joined two regional archaeological societies. Every month each society has a speaker about an archaeological topic. Collectively, they put on a happy face and using a PowerPoint presentation, each focuses on new and exciting archaeology in Florida. At our May 2018 meeting, a historian presented to a packed room the State of Florida's new, exciting, and "globally important" underwater site. Typical of all these dumbed-down presentations for the public, I learned nothing additional that I had not already learned by the dozens of feature articles in national newspapers, about the findings that is. Further questioning of the speaker revealed that despite the State of Florida's pronouncements and press releases about the global importance of the Manasota Offshore site excavation by diver/archaeologists, the state's enthusiasm was not matched in funding. Questioning revealed the state of archaeology in the United States in the twentieth century: no money.

While conducting my research, I contacted many of the anthropologists and archaeologists referenced in my book. A common response to my request was that they did not have the time to pursue the subject. Lately I have learned that not enough time is archaeological speak for there's no money in it. Of course, any student who chooses anthropology as their major in college should know that in terms of a return on their investment, law, medicine, and engineering all provide considerably more income as a profession. Since 1949, anyone pursuing a career in anthropology and archaeology have had a career as academics, and it has been their salaries as professors that paid the rent. Most students and graduate students similarly avoid education since teachers make less money than lawyers, doctors, and engineers. With a few exceptions, the majority of researchers after 1918 who conducted research and are referenced in my book is or was a professor. The term *ivory tower* more than adequately describes the keepers of prehistoric knowledge and theory in Florida and the United States since 1949. The public, who should be the beneficiaries of that prehistoric knowledge, have been locked out. As I will explain, this is a regrettable, unnecessary, and suicidal state of affairs. There is no sign that governments will find the time or the money to foster archaeological research and the protection and development of prehistoric sites for future generations. Therefore, in order to prevent the end of such and provide for a future, private/public partnerships will be necessary. In order to advantage the benefits of private/public partnerships, the folks in the ivory tower must meet us on a level and shared playing field.

The historian in me believes that this is the time to look at the history of archaeology, or better, the history of the funding of, or the economics behind, archaeology. I began this journey into the Calusa with Frank Hamilton Cushing. Cushing was one of a few fairly wealthy, very eccentric, socially connected lovers of antiquities. By 1918, the person who was responsible for the greatest number of detailed excavations on the Florida Gulf Coast was a Philadelphian millionaire, Clarence B. Moore, who used his family wealth searching for antiquities around the world. Moore and Cushing were but two of dozens of wealthy philanthropists who pursued their passion for archaeology. They did not get rich from that activity. They had to be rich in order to pursue it. While I am sure they kept several for themselves, they believed in the social good and proceeded to build collections for museums for the study and enjoyment of future generations. Except for the Smithsonian Institution in Washington, DC, it was not government money but rather private funding that resulted in the archaeological excavations that supplied museums (also, privately funded) with their incredible collections of artifacts. Regarding South Florida, did you know that Palm Beach has one of the greatest number of billionaires in the world?

After 1929, philanthropy obviously declined. Big government, not because of a similar love for antiquities, took on the lion's share of public projects that included archaeological excavations in order to put people to work. As I wrote in chapter 3, Florida was a beneficiary of much of the federal infusion of funds into public archaeology. With World War II, it all came to an abrupt stop. The end of the brief but productive federally sponsored archaeology was picked up by the States. In Florida, the state was developing a system of roads and state parks. In Florida, there were so many prehistoric Indian sites that with every new state park came new findings and a need to professionally excavate those sites. The universities then played and continue to play the critical role.

Since the shift away from government funding for public archaeology, the number of prehistoric sites in Florida has increased by 1000 percent. I presently live in Charlotte County. In 1949, there were five known prehistoric sites. According to a recent request for information, there are 205 known sites in Charlotte County, some Archaic and the others either Manasota or Calusa. Not only are there no plans to research those sites, there are no zoning laws to protect them and no planning documents to list them as critical cultural resources. The five known sites have been totally destroyed by grave robbers. The implications for the future of archaeology and of these critical public prehistoric cultural resources is clear. It is not a very good picture. It was a recreational diver, the public, that found the barnacle-encrusted human jaw bone off Manasota Key, that caused the state to lock down the underwater site, initiate research, and threaten any would-be visitors with prosecution. It is now the individual diver/archaeologists who use their own money and uncompensated time to conduct the excavation and report the findings. The state won't even supply them with a boat, fuel, or dive equipment. Important to any archaeology, they have to come up with thousands of dollars to pay a lab for carbon dating their finds. They expect the residents near the shore to daily patrol the site a keep boaters and divers away from the site. Likewise, Florida universities have not offered any funds. The bottom line then is that the private parties are funding the excavation of the site while the government and universities control the excavation and take the credit. Excuse me for not volunteering. Insult to injury, the findings, the important details from this "globally significant site," will never reach the public. Even if someday the findings are written, they will be written for fellow scientists, in the sacred language only spoken by the academics. That is because there is no money in publishing those details. I mean they don't have the "time" to publish those details.

Continuing the present state of denial will prove to inadequately address the need for change. As a discussed in chapter 11, I believe that state, county, and local governments can be convinced to do the right thing when the public and their lobbying nonprofits show them the economic benefits of prehistoric sites as heritage tourism destinations. If using this new model, more public dollars taken from tourism taxes become available to archaeologists, archaeologists

Figure 13.1. Archaeologist brushing dirt off of ceramic sherd. istock.com.

can work. Archaeologists will need to change their act and communicate their work in forms that will be understood by the public and the public agencies. There will be as a result more accountability. For instance, if an archaeologist comes along and asks for public funds to research the dental hygiene of the Mayaimi people, they will be referred elsewhere. While I would never advocate for a system that would dumb down the research of prehistoric people, I likewise feel that far too often nonessential research attracts funds that would best serve more important work. If this book has emphasized one thing over another, it has been common sense. Common sense has never been the interest of big government or big universities.

If my research has shown me anything, it is that there is much more work to be done in order to understand and fully appreciate the hunter-gatherer prehistory of South Florida. I have been careful at every juncture to draw attention to the specific needs for further research. I have been careful to illustrate just where future research is necessary to verify or dispute theories and conclusions. This vital research will require not only new excavations but also redating of previous finds. All of this will require funds. All of this will require a direction and commitment by the researchers and the public agencies responsible for the research. All of this will require a departure from previous modes in that it must include educating the public and bringing them into the process as willing and informed partners. Public education in order to enlist the public into an advocacy and public partnership with prehistoric cultural resources is as radical as you can advocate today. I was very encouraged by the efforts of the University of West Florida when they developed the Florida Public Archaeology Network in the past decade. In their mission statement was included public outreach and taking archaeology to the schools. What has evolved, however, would never address the needs as stated in this book. The network's projects include so many historical periods that the most endangered early Indian sites get ignored. Far worse is that the network is run entirely by liberal academics, who use history to advance their agenda. Recently a regional director gave a talk about global warming and racism.

For decades now, states and communities on the coasts have had to deal with the Public Trust Doctrine, a US doctrine that has its source in British common law. The Public Trust Doctrine recognizes that the public has rights of access to coastal areas and beaches. The doctrine acknowledges that if allowed, certain humans would purchase and make private properties on the coast and that that would ultimately make access by the public impossible. Florida adopted the doctrine; thus, the public has always had access to the beaches and water. What I am advocating is that key environmental and cultural resources need to be similarly protected and made accessible to the public. Just as the coastal waters are in a public trust, so too are the environmental and cultural heritage sites. The billionaires who are buying and building in the gated community on Horr's Island should not privately hold the five-thousand-year-old mounds and shell ring on that site. First, there is plenty of land on the island for that use. Common sense and common law should dictate that a site that has the oldest burial mound in North America trumps one person's need for a vacation property. As if the Collier family needed more money, Collier and his family sold off every major Calusa site within several decades. If you want to know why there is so little data on the Calusa, there is your answer. Once property is sold to private concerns, without the implementation of the Public Trust Doctrine, the property is outside of the public trust. Occasionally, as in the case of Spanish Point in Sarasota County, the site is excavated, developed, and then donated to the public by the land owner, but very rarely.

There will come a point, probably in the next two decades, when the wealth of prehistoric archaeological sites in Florida diminish to a very few. Considering the lack of public education, the demise will come and go without any public notice. The public will not be upset about a loss of public cultural resources that were unfamiliar to them. Those people in Florida will just have to journey out of state to experience the real thing.

I know there are people out there that share my interest in prehistory. I have met them on my many journeys here and abroad. Tourism statistics likewise show an increase, and not a decrease, in both heritage as well as eco-tourism destinations. But ultimately, it will come down to educating the current and future generations. I grew up with parents that demonstrated to us the value of such resources. While a student, teachers took us to places of historical significance. Perhaps, then, that is what is broken. Our culture, and specifically our culture in Florida, is failing us. What can one person do? First, stay informed. Read about the people and cultures and the prehistory that interests you. Compare and contrast the research completed. If you have children or grandchildren, share your interest with them. Do not be selfish. If you discover a valuable prehistoric site is in danger, speak out. Be informed about the site and contact the elected and appointed officials who can make a difference. Write a letter to the editor. By all means, do not be intimidated or dismissed. That is why the more you study, you will have the power that comes from knowledge. Be supportive. If you like what a particular anthropologist or archaeologist has done, search online for their email and show support for their work.

If like me, you already do these things and make the time to be involved exploring the mysteries of the past, you might be considering taking your passion to the next level. The issue of funding must be addressed, and sooner rather than later. I am already involved in contacting commissioners as well as chambers of commerce and economic development groups about the possibilities of heritage tourism. The key is to convince those who can access the revenues from tourism taxes to use them for the development of an archaeological site to be developed as a tourist destination. I use the Poverty Point site as my model. Unlike 99 percent of significant archaeological sites, the Louisiana Department of State, rather than discourage the public, as they do in Florida, will, after excavating the site, develop it as a tourist designation. As a result, Poverty Point is now a United Nations World Heritage site. The site that now attracts visitors from around the world supports archaeologists and a variety of jobs and businesses.

My research on heritage and eco-tourism has shown that when a state or country invests in this worthy type of project, there is typically a five-to-one return. For every dollar spent on development and maintenance of the site or park, five in income is derived. My research of sites in Florida shows that once a site is excavated, it has a 99 percent chance of being destroyed. The researchers who were the only people to have access, after getting what they wanted, felt no responsibility to preserve and protect the site for others. Along with the State of Florida, the archaeologists are so fearful of vandalism, their very behaviors actually increase the chances for vandalism or worse, since the sites are kept secret. The public who could mobilize for their preservation cannot possibly do so since they have no idea that they existed in the first place. Referring back to the false promise of the Florida Public Archaeology Network, every year they train "scouts." Scouts are local volunteers who must sign a pledge not to disclose the location of a site. Their job is to report on the condition of one, or several, of the archaeological sites on the state's master file. The program has had a net effect. Over the past decade, not one site has been protected. I have repeatedly called the director for the region that hosts the Fort Center site to have them do the work to have the site designated as a National Historic Landmark. She never returns my calls. Common sense would tell you secrecy has resulted in the destruction of sites. Insanity is doing the same thing, over and over again, when it is apparent that it doesn't work.

The truth about the protection of prehistoric sites is that once you educate the public, once you involve them in the process and acknowledge the fact that they are in the "public trust," the public will protect what is rightfully theirs. Calusa archaeologist Theresa Schober recounts in her presentation how when the call went out for residents to assist with the excavation and research of a Calusa shell mound in Fort Myers Beach a few years back, hundreds of volunteers showed up. When a prehistoric site and its needs are made public, people respond out of interest, and they have the inclination to take pride in and protect what is rightfully theirs and held in common from thieves. I dare to say that they will do it far more effectively and efficiently than the state or local authorities. Currently, the officials, the researchers have neither the time nor the money, and the public as well. By removing these cultural resources from the public trust, by keeping them secret, they have assumed responsibility for them. They have claimed stewardship, a responsibility that they have demonstrated collectively they are ill equipped to manage.

Talk being cheap, when I was completing my research for this book in the summer of 2018, I put the word out on a Meetup.com site that I was starting a Charlotte Harbor Anthropological Society. The site now has over forty people, and twenty-four have joined as members of the society. Nearby in Venice, Florida, a local historical society decided to do monthly presentations on the prehistoric cultures in South Florida. So many people showed up that they were forced to send over two hundred away. The interest to learn is definitely there. I have great hope and a renewed sense of purpose to share the narrative of the mound-building epoch in South Florida and preserve its treasures for future generations.

Epilogue

In my preface, I wrote of my 1990 encounter with representatives of the indigenous cultures of northern Russia and the Far East. This was the first such encounter in world history between the native people of North America and those of Siberia. Even today, I am moved by their chance meeting and the implications for the future of our planet. After all, their ancestors were the ones who stayed behind in the ancestral lands fourteen thousand years ago in those northern regions above the Arctic circle. They made good choices and had successfully adapted. Each group found their niche and passed on their knowledge to the next generation. The conference was titled The Seventh Generation, for its organizers in the United States and the Soviet Union were concerned about what each great world power would pass on to future generations.

Long ago, some of these people who had adapted to the harsh Arctic environments moved east across the Bering Strait into North America. They were all nomadic hunters, but after the glaciers receded, new opportunities appeared, the lands warmed, and the seas rose, and their descendants settled down, descendants such as the Calusa and Mayaimi. They brought with them to each new home their language, their stories, their beliefs, and their making of sacred objects.

The people that I met in Moscow in 1990 shared their losses about their people, their language, religion, and way of life living under the Soviet State. Not unlike Native Americans a hundred years earlier, the young men were forced to leave their people and go to Soviet schools to be enculturated into the Soviet experiment. Few returned to their lands, people, and way of life. This led to the eventual destruction of many ancient cultures. During the Soviet experiment, shamanism was outlawed. The shaman was the group healer and medicine man or woman. In fact, the word *shaman* came from Siberia. With our group that traveled to Moscow that fall were a Sioux medicine man, a Cherokee shaman, and a Mohawk storyteller, who knew all too well the fate of these people of the northern lands. None of us knew, however, that in only two years the Soviet experiment would end. These ancient hunter-gatherers had been forced to abandon their way of life and adopt the Russian/Soviet culture and all of its "advancements." It was all for naught, since the utopian state failed after only seventy-five years, not even a century. The collapse of the Soviet Union was good news to the aboriginal people. While presently they struggle with the breakdowns in goods and services, their autonomy is no longer threatened. There is every indication that the majority of these cultures will survive into the twenty-first century.

This book focused on two fishing-hunter-gathering cultures who did not survive. Had any state attempted to remove them from their lands and take their young, they would have fought them to the end. History tells the story of hunter-gatherers that, once several generations discontinue the ways of the people and they abandon their language and beliefs, it is almost impossible to restore the original culture. Ten years before I met these seminomadic herdsmen studying in Moscow, 70 percent of the aboriginal people of the north were still living their traditional nomadic or seminomadic way of life. When the Soviet Union collapsed in 1982, it was less than 50 percent. Considering the history, 50 percent is a great deal more than none. Today, the Russian government recognizes and protects forty-one of these indigenous cultures that have fewer than fifty thousand people. Of the current forty-one groups, eleven live above the Arctic circle and have fewer than one thousand people. Recent statistics show that of these indigenous hunter-gatherers, they make up approximately 250,000 or 0.2 percent of the total population. Their lands, however, comprise two-thirds the total of Russian territory. These lands do contain resources desired by the state and multinational corporations. Therefore, future interactions and treaties will be more than likely not to their advantage.

In 1990, I enrolled in my first training in shamanism. My first teacher was a nonindigenous shaman, Michael Harner. Harner had studied shamanism past and present around the world. He wrote of his studies in *The Way of the Shaman* (1980). Based on his work, he founded the Foundation for Shamanic Studies. He trained teachers in "core shamanism," which now offers training globally for the past thirty-eight years. My training has significantly altered my worldview. Those insights helped me to formulate my research into the Calusa and Mayaimi people, especially in the subjects of sacred places and their beliefs and mythology. Because of Harner's work, shamanism has now returned to its place of origin, Siberia. Indigenous beliefs restored, these past decades have witnessed similar attacks by hostile governments in central and South America. This book is a homage to the legacy of hunter-gatherers. It is an attempt by one author to protect the record and to honor their persistence.

It amazes me that I find myself in 2018 trying to educate environmentalists and environmental agencies. No other group stands in the way of preserving and maintaining Florida's remaining sites, sites that are still in their original wilderness context, than the protectors of our "biological resources." They still view the world and the local environment using the Cartesian model. The task at hand, and it is critical to sustainability, is that we all revisit as often as possible these sites as landmarks of a time when human societies lived related to and in interrelation to all living things.

Bibliography

Allen, Ross. "The Big Circle Mounds." *Florida Anthropologist* (1948): 17–21.

Berry, Wendell. *What Are People For?* Berkeley, CA: Counterpoint, 1990.

Burkhart, Brian Yazzie. "What Coyote and Thales Can Teach Us: An Outline of American Indian Epistemology." In *American Indian Thought*, edited by Anne Waters, 15–26. Malden, MA: Blackwell, 2004.

Byers, A. Martin *The Real Mound Builders of North America: A Critical Realist Prehistory of the Eastern Woodlands, 200 BC–1450 AD*. Lanham, MD: Lexington Books, 2018.

Calver, James L. *Florida Kaolins and Clays*. Florida Geological Survey, Special Publication No. 35, 1949. http://publicfiles.dep.state.fl.us/FGS publication.

Capra, Fritjof. *The Turning Point: Science, Society and the Rising Culture*. New York: Bantam Books, 1982.

Carr, Robert S. "Prehistoric Circular Earthworks in South Florida." *Florida Anthropologist* (May 1985).

Clark, John E. "Surrounding the Sacred: Geometry and Design of Early Mound Groups as Meaning and Function." In Richard William Jefferies, *Signs of Power: The Rise of Cultural Complexity in the Southeast*. Tuscaloosa: University of Alabama Press, 2004.

Cushing, Frank Hamilton. "Key Marco Types." Unpublished manuscript, National Anthropological Archives, Washington, DC: Smithsonian Institution.

———. *The Lost Manuscripts of Frank Hamilton Cushing*, edited by Phyllis Kolianos and Brent R. Weisman. Gainesville: University Press of Florida, [1896] 2005.

Dilts, Robert. *Changing Belief Systems with NLP*. Capitola, CA: Meta Publications, 1990.

Dye, David H., and Adam King. "Desecrating the Sacred Ancestor Temples: Chiefly Conflict and Violence in the American Southeast." In Richard J. Chacon and Rubén G. Mendoza, *North American Indigenous Warfare and Ritula Violence*. Tucson: University of Arizona Press, 2007.

Ehmann, Ted. *Investigating the Existence of Clay Beds Sourced by the Aboriginal People for Ceramic Production in Central and South Florida*. Charlotte Harbor Anthropological Society Publications, http://charlotteharboras.org, 2018.

———. *Stealing Their Thunder: Dealing Out the Calusa and Their Role in the Cultural Manifestation in Southern Florida during the Woodland Periods*. Charlotte Harbor Anthropological Society Publications, http://charlotteharboras.org, 2018.

———. *Unthinkable Acts of Violence: Archaeological Evidence of an Intentional Raid and Desecration of the Mortuary Complex at Fort Center, AD 700–AD 900*. Charlotte Harbor Anthropological Society Publications, http://charlotteharboras.org, 2018.

Escalante Fontaneda, Hernando de. *Memoir of de Escalante Fontaneda Respecting Florida, Written in Spain about the Year 1575*, trans. by Buckingham Smith and with editorial comments by D. O. True. Coral Gables, FL: Glades House, 1973.

Fox, Robin. *The Challenge of Anthropology: Old Encounters and New Excursions*. New Brunswick, NJ: Transaction Press, 1994.

Gibson, Jon L. *The Ancient Mounds of Poverty Point: Place of Rings*. Gainesville: University Press of Florida, 2001.

———. "The Power of Beneficent Obligation in the First Mound-Building Societies." In *Signs of Power: The Rise of Cultural Complexity in the Southeast*, edited by Jon L. Gibson and Philip J. Carr. Tuscaloosa: University of Alabama Press, 2004.

Gilliland, Marion Spjut. *The Calusa Indians of Florida*. M.S. Gilliland, 1996.

———. *Key Marco's Buried Treasure: Archaeology and Adventure in the Nineteenth Century*. Gainesville: University Press of Florida, 1989.

———. *The Material Culture of Key Marco, Florida*. Port Salerno, FL: Sunshine Books, 1989.

Goggin, John M. *The Archaeology of the Glades Area, Southern Florida*. Gainesville: University of Florida, 1949.

———. "Florida Archaeology–1950." *The Florida Anthropologist* (May 1950).

———. "A Preliminary Definition of Archaeological Areas and Periods in Florida," in *Indian and Spanish Writings*, edited by Charles H. Fairbanks, Irving Rouse, and William C. Sturtevant. Coral Gables, FL: University of Miami Press, 1964.

Granberry, Julian. *The Calusa: Linguistic and Cultural Origins and Relationships*. Tuscaloosa: University of Alabama Press, 2011.

Harner, Michael. *The Way of the Shaman*. New York: Harper One, 1980.

Johnson, William G. "The Role of Maize in South Florida Aboriginal Societies: An Overview." *Florida Anthropologist* (May 1990).

Lawres, Nathan R. *Materializing Ontology in Monumental Form: Engaging the Ontological in the Okeechobee Basin, FL*. Chicago, IL: University of Chicago Press, 2017.

Lawres, Nathan, and Matthew H. Colvin. "Presenting the First Chronometric Dates from Big Mound City, Florida." *Florida Anthropologist* 70, nos. 1–2 (2017).

Little, Gregory J., *The Illustrated Encyclopedia of Native American Mounds & Earthworks*. Memphis, TN: Eagle Wing Books, 2009.

Luer, George M. "Calusa Canals in Southwestern Florida: Routes of Tribute and Exchange." *Florida Anthropologist* 4, no. 2 (June 1989).

———. "Three Metal Ceremonial Tablets with Comments on the Tampa Bay Area." *Florida Anthropologist* 5, no. 1 (March 2000).

Luer, George M., and Marion M. Almy. "A Defining of the Manasota Culture." *Florida Anthropologist* 35, no. 1 (March 1982).

Luer, George M., et al. "The Myakkahatchee Site: A Large Multi-Period Inland from Shore Site, Sarasota County, Florida." *Florida Anthropologist* 4, no. 1 (1987).

MacMahon, Darcie A., and William H. Marquardt. *The Calusa and Their LegacY: South Florida People and Their Environments.* Gainesville: University Press of Florida, 2004.

Marquardt, William H. "The Emergence and Demise of the Calusa." In *Societies in Eclipse: Archaeology of the Eastern Woodland Indians, A.D. 1400–1700*, ed. David S. Brose et al. Washington, DC: Smithsonian Institution, 2001.

———. "Tracking the Calusa: A Retrospect." *Southeastern Archaeology* 33, no. 1 (2014).

Marquardt, William H., and Karen Walker. *The Archaeology of Pineland: A Coastal Southwest Flordia Site Complex, A. D. 50–1710.* Gainesville: University Press of Florida, 2013.

McGoun, William E. *Prehistoric Peoples of South Florida.* Tuscaloosa, GA: University of Alabama Press, 1994.

Milanich, Jerald T. *Archaeology of Precolumbian Florida.* Gainesville: University Press of Florida, 1993.

———. *Florida's Indians from Ancient Times to the Present.* Gainesville: University Press of Florida, 1998.

Milner, George R. "Warfare, Population, and Food Production in Prehistoric Eastern North America." In *North American Indigenous Warfare and Ritual Violence*, edited by Richard J. Chacon and Ruben G. Mendoza. Tucson: University of Arizona Press, 2013.

Mitchem, Jeffrey McClain. *Redefining Safety Harbor: Late Prehistoric/Protohistoric Archaeology in West Peninsular Florida.* Gainesville: University of Florida Dissertation, 1989.

———. *The West and Central Florida Expeditions of Clarence Bloomfield Moore,* Tuscaloosa: University of Alabama Press, 1999.

Moore, Clarence Bloomfield. *The West and Central Florida Expeditions of Clarence Bloomfield Moore*, edited by Jeffrey M. Mitchem. Tuscaloosa: University of Alabama Press, 1908.

Pluckhahn, Thomas, *Kolomoki: Settlement, Cheremony, and Status in the Deep South, A. D. 350 to 750.* Tuscaloosa: University of Alabama Press, 2003.

———. "The Sacred and the Secular Revisited." In *Becoming Villages, Comparing Early Village Societies*, edited by Matthew S. Bandy and Jake R. Fox. Tucson: University of Arizona Press, 2010.

Pozorski, Sheila, and Thomas Pozorski. *Early Settlement and Subsistence in the Casma Valley, Peru.* Iowa City: University of Iowa Press, 1987.

Russo, Michael. *Archaic Sedentism on the Florida Coast.* Gainesville: University of Florida Graduate Dissertation, 1991.

———. "Measuring Shell Rings for Social Inequality." In *Signs of Power*, edited by John L. Gibson and Philip Carr. Tuscaloosa, AL: University of Alabama Press, 2004.

Sawyer, Wells Moses. *Florida Notebook.* Gainesville: University of Florida Library Digital Collection.

Schober, Theresa. "Deconstructing and Reconstructing Caloosahatchee Shell Mound Building." In *New Histories of Pre-Columbian Florida*, edited by Neill J. Wallis and Asa R. Randall. Gainesville: University Press of Florida, 2014.

Sears, William H. "Cape Coral Sites." *Florida Anthropologist* (1964).

———. *Fort Center: An Archaeological Site in the Lake Okeechobee Basin*. Gainesville: University Press of Florida, 1982.

Swan, James A. *Sacred Places: How the Living Earth Seeks Our Friendship*. Santa Fe, NM: Bear & Company, 1990.

Thompson, Victor D., and Thomas J. Pluckhahn. "Constituting Similarity and Difference in the Deep South: The Ritual and Domestic Landscapes of Kolomoki, Crystal River, and Fort Center." In *Early and Middle Woodland Landscapes of the Southeast*, edited by Alice P. Wright. Gainesville: University Press of Florida, 2013.

———. "The Modification and Manipulation of Landscape at Fort Center." In *New Histories of Precolumbian Florida*, edited by Neill J. Wallis and Asa R. Randall, 163–79. Gainesville: University Press Scholarship, 2014.

———. "Monumentalization of the Ritual Landscapes at Fort Center in the Lake Okeechobee Basin in South Florida." *Journal of Anthropological Archaeology* 31 (2013): 49–65.

Turner, Victor. *The Ritual Process*. New York: Aline De Gruyter, 1960.

Wheeler, Ryan J. "The Ortona Canals: Aboriginal Canal Hydraulics and Engineering." *Florida Anthropologist* 48, no. 4 (December 1995).

———. *Treasure of the Calusa: The Johnson/Willcox Collection from Mound Key, Florida*. Tallahassee: Rose Printing, 2000.

Wheeler, Ryan J., and Robert S. Carr, "It's Ceremonial, Right?" in *New Histories of Pre-Columbian Florida*. Gainesville: University of Florida Press, 2014.

Widmer, Randolph J. *The Evolution of CalusA: A Nonagricultural Chiefdom on the Southwest Flordia Coast*. Tuscaloosa: University of Alabama Press, 1988.

Willey, Gordon R. *Archaeology of the Florida Gulf Coast*. Washington, DC: The Smithsonian Institution, 1949.

Wood, Michael. *Legacy: The Search for Ancient Cultures*. New York: Sterling Press, 1995.

Index

About the Author

Ted Ehmann lives in Port Charlotte, Florida, and is the founder and president of the Charlotte County Anthropological Society. He did not intend to be an author, faced with the discoveries he made while researching the prehistory of his new home; but he was compelled to share his findings to a larger audience. Because *The People of the Great Circle* incorporates a call to action, he proceeded in June 2018 to create a regional anthropological society that has a mission statement that mirrors the rethinking of the prehistoric epoch in south Florida. The society website, https://charlotteharboras.org provides information on all new and advancing research. For the first time in the history of North American anthropology, there is a website dedicated to South Florida prehistory and mound builders. The site is a clearing house for presentations, field trips, research, and festivals devoted to these prehistoric mound builders in South Florida.